Level
1

Activities
for a
Differentiated
Classroom

Developed by

Wendy Conklin, M.A.

 SHELL EDUCATION

247 061

Consultant

Chandra C. Prough, M.S.Ed.
National Board Certified
Newport-Mesa
Unified School District

Contributing Authors

Amy Griffing

Publishing Credits

Dona Herweck Rice, *Editor-in-Chief;* Lee Aucoin, *Creative Director;*
Don Tran, *Print Production Manager;* Timothy J. Bradley, *Illustration Manager;*
Chris McIntyre, M.A.Ed., *Editorial Director;* Sara Johnson, M.S.Ed., *Senior Editor;*
Aubrie Nielsen, M.S., *Associate Education Editor;* Robin Erickson, *Interior Layout Designer;*
Juan Chavolla, *Production Artist;* Stephanie Reid, *Photo Editor;*
Corinne Burton, M.S.Ed., *Publisher*

Image Credits

p.114 (top left) Michal Ninger/Shutterstock, (top right) John A. Anderson/Shutterstock, (bottom left) Vadim Davydov/Shutterstock, (bottom right) Aynia Brennan/Shutterstock; p.156 Getty Images; p.157 Getty Images; p.163 Library of Congress [LC-USZC4-9905]; p.165 (top left) Carl Lindberg/wikimedia, (top right) Jacobolus/wikimedia, (bottom left) Yaddah Hoshie/wikimedia, (bottom right) Jacobolus/wikimedia

Shell Education
5301 Oceanus Drive
Huntington Beach, CA 92649-1030
http://www.shelleducation.com
ISBN 978-1-4258-0733-7
©2011 Shell Educational Publishing, Inc.

Table of Contents

Introduction

Language Arts Lessons

Mathematics Lessons

Science Lessons

Social Studies Lessons

Appendices

Understanding Differentiation

As I conduct workshops with teachers of all ages and grade levels, I hear a familiar tune: *Differentiating curriculum is worrisome and stressful.* I believe this is due to the fact that teachers do not know how to begin differentiating. Their administrators tell them that they must differentiate, but teachers are overwhelmed with the task of doing it because there is not a clear explanation of what to do. Teachers know the theory. They know they need to do it. They just do not know *how* to do it.

The right way to differentiate depends on the unique students in a classroom. To successfully differentiate, teachers must first know their students. Knowing where students are academically helps us understand where to begin. When we have students who do not succeed, we need to find out why they are not succeeding. Then, we look for the kinds of support that they need to help them learn specific concepts. We make adjustments when students have trouble comprehending material. We look for new ways to present information, new manipulatives that make sense, and opportunities to provide additional support. As our struggling students grow, we can then reduce the amount of support that we provide so that students continue to grow instead of leaning too heavily on that support. Differentiation is about meeting the needs of *all* students and providing the right amount of challenge for *all* students.

What Should I Differentiate and Why?

Many teachers have heard the terms *content*, *process*, and *product* when it comes to differentiating curriculum, but few have the time to ponder how these words apply to what they do in their classrooms. Below is a chart that quickly defines how we differentiate and why we differentiate.

Differentiating Curriculum

How	Why
Vary the Content (what is taught)	**Readiness** (students are not at the same place academically)
Vary the Process (how it is taught)	**Learning Styles** (students prefer different ways of learning)
Vary the Product (what students produce)	**Interests** (students have different passions)

Differentiation Strategies in This Book

What Differentiation Strategies Can I Use?

Each book in the *Activities for a Differentiated Classroom* series introduces a selection of differentiation strategies. Each lesson in this book uses one of the six differentiation strategies outlined below. The strategies are used across different curriculum areas and topics to provide you with multiple real-world examples.

Differentiation Strategy		Lessons in This Book
	Tiered Assignments	• Reading for Fluency—*Language Arts* • Extending Patterns—*Mathematics* • Water Changes—*Science* • Chinese New Year—*Social Studies*
	Three-Story Intellect	• Memories—*Language Arts* • Measurement—*Mathematics* • Weather—*Science* • Changes in Community—*Social Studies*
	Multiple Intelligences	• Retelling—*Language Arts* • Fractions!—*Mathematics* • Where Does the Moon Go?—*Science* • On the Trail—*Social Studies*
	Menu of Options	• Descriptive Words—*Language Arts* • Time—*Mathematics* • Scientists Observe and Experiment!—*Science* • Alexander Graham Bell—*Social Studies*
	Open-Ended Tasks	• Poetry—*Language Arts* • Geometry—*Mathematics* • Plants—*Science* • Family Life and Community—*Social Studies*
	Leveled Learning Centers	• Words Are Everywhere—*Language Arts* • More-or-Less Story Problems—*Mathematics* • How Do Birds Eat?—*Science* • American Symbols—*Social Studies*

Differentiation Strategies in This Book *(cont.)*

Tiered Assignments

One way to ensure that all students in a classroom advance—using the same skills and ideas regardless of readiness levels—is to tier lessons. Often referred to as *scaffolding*, tiered assignments offer multilevel activities based on key skills at differing levels of complexity. One example of this is leveled reading texts. All students can learn about the Civil War by reading texts that are leveled according to the different reading abilities in the classroom. You can also provide comprehension questions that are leveled. Each student comes away with essential grade-appropriate skills in addition to being sufficiently challenged. The entire class works toward one goal (learning about the Civil War), but the path to that goal depends on each student's readiness level.

So, how do you tier lessons?

- **Pick the skill, concept, or strategy that needs to be learned.** For example, a key concept would be using reading skills and strategies to understand and interpret a variety of informational texts.

- **Think of an activity that teaches this skill, concept, or strategy.** For this example, you could have students summarize the information and include a main idea in the summary.

- **Assess students.** You may already have a good idea of your students' readiness levels, but you can further assess them through classroom discussions, quizzes, tests, or journal entries. These assessments can tell you if students are above grade level, on grade level, or below grade level.

- **Take another look at the activity you developed.** How complex is it? Where would it fit on a continuum scale? Is it appropriate for above-grade-level learners, on-grade-level learners, below-grade-level learners, or English language learners?

- **Modify the activity to meet the needs of the other learners in the class.** Try to get help from the specialists in your school for English language learners, special education students, and gifted learners. For this example, summarizing with a main idea would be appropriate for on-grade-level students. Above-grade-level students should include supporting details in their summaries. The below-grade-level students will need a few examples provided for their summaries. English language learners will begin with the same examples given to below-grade-level students so that they understand what is expected of them. Then, they will summarize information verbally to you.

Remember, just because students are above grade level does not mean that they should be given more work. And, just because students are below grade level does not mean that they should be given less work. Tiered lessons are differentiated by varying the *complexity*, not necessarily the *quantity* of work required for the assignment. Likewise, all tiered activities should be interesting and engaging.

Differentiation Strategies in This Book *(cont.)*

Three-Story Intellect

> "There are one-story intellects, two-story intellects, and three-story intellects with skylights. All fact collectors who have no aim beyond their facts are one-story people. Two-story people compare, reason, and generalize, using labors of fact collectors as well as their own. Three-story people idealize, imagine, and predict. Their best illuminations come from above through the skylight."

This quotation is from Oliver Wendell Holmes, a physician and author who lived in the 1800s. Art Costa applied Holmes's quote to academics and produced the three-story intellect model (Costa and Marzano 1987). This model categorizes thinking into three levels. The three levels work together to process information much like the brain works. First, the brain gathers information, then processes it for understanding, and finally applies the information.

Level I, called the **Gathering** or **Input Phase**, describes how students gather information through their senses. This is the foundation for higher-level thinking. Students learn to state problems in their own words, observe and gather information for making decisions, create goals, and connect information with previous experiences.

Level II is the **Processing Phase**. Information is processed to make it meaningful. Students build on the foundation of skills in Level I by comparing, inferring, organizing, and questioning information.

In **Level III**, the **Applying Phase**, students incorporate all the levels of thinking. They generate new ideas by predicting, judging, imagining, and evaluating.

It is not necessary to advance our thinking in a particular order. Thinking can begin at any level. For example, if you give students a problem to solve, they are beginning at Level III. A problematic situation is one of the best ways to get students excited about learning. When students are confronted with a problem (Level III), they must gather information (Level I), process it (Level II), and then return to the problem (Level III) to make a final decision.

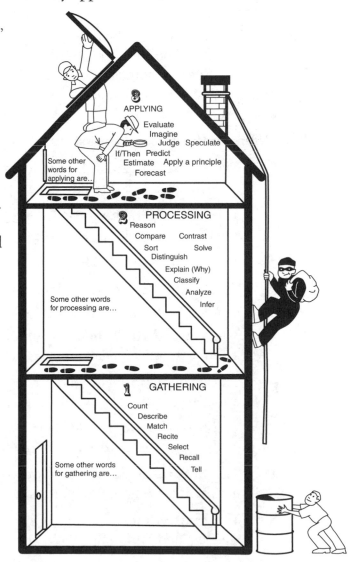

Differentiation Strategies in This Book *(cont.)*

Multiple Intelligences

The multiple-intelligences model is based on the work of Howard Gardner (1983). He has identified nine intelligences, which include verbal/linguistic, logical/mathematical, visual/spatial, bodily/kinesthetic, musical/rhythmic, interpersonal, intrapersonal, naturalist, and existential. Gardner says that everyone possesses each of these intelligences, but in each of us, some intelligences are more developed than others.

Some research suggests that certain pathways of learning are stronger at certain stages of development. Sue Teele (1994) devised a survey titled the "Teele Inventory for Multiple Intelligences." She gave it to more than 6,000 students. Her research found that verbal/linguistic intelligence is strongest in kindergarten through third grade. It declines dramatically thereafter. The logical/mathematical intelligence is strongest in first through fourth grade. It also declines dramatically thereafter. The visual/spatial and bodily/kinesthetic intelligences were shown to be dominant throughout elementary and middle school. In addition, middle-school children also show a preference for musical/rhythmic and interpersonal intelligences. Teele's findings show that if elementary teachers want to use the best strategies, they must present lessons that incorporate verbal/linguistic, logical/mathematical, visual/spatial, and bodily/kinesthetic activities.

The Nine Multiple Intelligences

- The **Verbal/Linguistic** child thinks in words. This child likes to write, read, play word games, and tell interesting stories.

- The **Logical/Mathematical** child thinks by reasoning. This child likes finding solutions to problems, solving puzzles, experimenting, and calculating.

- The **Visual/Spatial** child thinks in pictures. This child likes to draw and design.

- The **Bodily/Kinesthetic** child thinks by using the body. This child likes dancing, moving, jumping, running, and touching.

- The **Musical/Rhythmic** child thinks in melodies and rhythms. This child likes listening to music, making music, tapping to the rhythm, and singing.

- The **Interpersonal** child thinks by talking about ideas with others. This child likes organizing events, being the leader, mediating between friends, and celebrating.

- The **Intrapersonal** child keeps thoughts to him- or herself. This child likes to set goals, meditate, daydream, and be in quiet places.

- The **Naturalist** child thinks by classifying. This child likes studying anything in nature, including rocks, animals, plants, and the weather.

- The **Existential** child reflects inwardly about the ultimate issues in life while learning and interacting with others. This child likes to express opinions.

Differentiation Strategies in This Book *(cont.)*

Menu of Options

Providing students the opportunity to choose what activity they want to do increases their level of interest in what they are doing or learning. However, many students do not often get the chance to make choices about their work. It can be challenging and time-consuming for teachers to develop a variety of engaging activities. Yet offering options is essential to getting students interested and motivated in learning. When students are involved in something of their own choosing, they are more engaged in the learning process (Bess 1997; Brandt 1998).

Choices in the classroom can be offered in a variety of ways. Students can choose what they will learn (content), how they will learn (process), and how they will show what they have learned (product). A menu of options is a strategy that differentiates product by giving students the opportunity to choose from a list of highly engaging activities.

The menu of options strategy works well for many reasons. First, it operates much like a menu from a restaurant. A person looking at a menu sees all the choices. Some cost more and some cost less. No one likes going to a restaurant and being told what to eat. People enjoy choosing what they prefer from the menu. In the same way, a menu of options offers students many different projects from which to choose. These projects are assigned various point values. The point values depend on the amount of work or detail involved in the project. Students must earn a set number of points determined by the teacher, but they can choose which activities they want to complete. Any kind of point system can be used. For example, basic projects that do not take much time can be worth 10 points. Projects that take a moderate amount of time and energy can be worth 30 points. Projects that are very time-consuming can be worth 50 points. If the students need to complete 80 points total, they can get to that total number in many different ways. They may choose a 50-point project and a 30-point project. Or, they may choose two 30-point projects and two 10-point projects.

Secondly, a menu of options is effective because the freedom of choice allows students to complete projects that are of interest to them. This increases the chance that the students will produce high-quality products. Students like to feel in control. When given a list to choose from, students often choose projects that they like or that fit their learning styles. If the teacher provides enough variety, then all students can find projects that they feel passionate about.

As an alternative to creating a menu of options based on point systems, a teacher can create three or four sections on a menu of options and ask students to choose one project from each section. This strategy is helpful when there are a particular set of concepts that the teacher needs to be sure that students have learned.

Grouping Students *(cont.)*

What Grouping Strategies Can I Use? *(cont.)*

Flexogeneous Grouping

Flexogeneous grouping allows for the flexible grouping of homogeneous and heterogeneous groups within the same lesson. Students switch groups at least one time during the lesson to create another group. For example, the homogeneous groups meet for half the lesson and then switch to form heterogeneous groups for the rest of the lesson.

One easy flexogeneous grouping strategy is to jigsaw or mix up already established homogeneous groups. To jigsaw groups, allow homogeneous groups of students to work together for part of the lesson (circle, square, and triangle groups). Then, distinguish group members by labeling them *A*, *B*, and *C* within the same group. All the *A*s form a new group, the *B*s form a new group, and the *C*s form a new group.

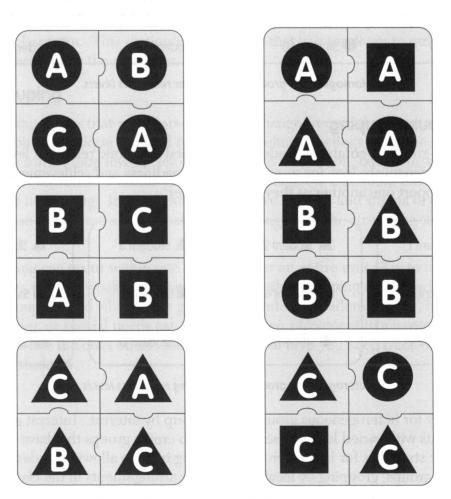

Flexogeneous grouping uses homogeneous and heterogeneous groups in a single lesson.

Working with English Language Learners

Strategies for Working with English Language Learners

Use visual media as an alternative to written responses. Have all students express their thinking through visual media, such as drawings, posters, or slide shows. This is an effective strategy for eliciting responses from English language learners. This also fosters creativity in all students, challenges above-grade-level students, provides opportunities for artistically inclined students who may struggle academically, and avoids singling out English language learners.

Frame questions to make the language accessible. At times, you will need to rephrase questions to clarify meaning for English language learners. Framing questions makes the language accessible to all students. Higher-order questions can be asked without reducing their rigor. Pose questions for English language learners with question stems or frames.

Example Question Stems/Frames

- What would happen if…?
- What is your opinion?
- Why do you think…?
- How would you prove…?
- Would it be better if…?

- How is _____ related to _____?
- If you could _____, what would you do?
- Can you invent _____?
- Why is _____ important?
- Why is _____ better than _____?

Give context to questions to enable understanding. This can be done by placing pictures or small icons directly next to key words. English language learners also benefit from chunking sentences. For example, with the question *In the ocean, how do wind and ocean currents make boats move?* English language learners can see right away that the question is about the ocean, so they have a context for answering the question.

Provide English language learners with sentence stems or frames to encourage higher-order thinking. These learners need language tools to help them express what they think. Sentence stems or frames will not only get the information you need and want from your English language learners, but it will also model how they should be speaking. You can provide these sentence stems or frames on small sticky notes for students to keep at their desks, or write them on laminated cards and distribute them to students when necessary.

Example Sentence Stems/Frames

- This is important because…
- This is better because…
- This is similar because…
- This is different because…

- I agree with _____ because…
- I disagree with _____ because…
- I think _____ because…
- I think _____ will happen because…

Partner up, and let partners share aloud. Have English language learners work with language-proficient students to answer questions, solve problems, or create projects. Language-proficient partners can provide the academic vocabulary needed to express ideas. Prepare your language-proficient students to work with language learners by explaining that they must speak slowly and clearly and give these learners time to think and speak.

Working with English Language Learners *(cont.)*

How Can I Support English Language Learners?

All teachers should know the language-acquisition level of each of their English language learners. Knowing these levels will help to plan instruction. Using visuals to support oral and written language for students at Level 1 will help make the language more comprehensible. Students at Levels 2 and 3 benefit from pair work in speaking tasks, but they will need additional individual support during writing and reading tasks. Students at Levels 4 and 5 may still struggle with comprehending the academic language used during instruction, as well as with reading and writing. Use the chart below to plan appropriate questions and activities.

Proficiency Levels for English Language Learners—Quick Glance

Proficiency Level	Questions to Ask	Activities/Actions		
Level 1—Entering • minimal comprehension • no verbal production	• Where is…? • What is the main idea? • What examples do you see? • What are the parts of…? • What would happen if…? • What is your opinion?	• listen • point	• draw • circle	• mime
Level 2—Beginning • limited comprehension • short spoken phrases	• Can you list three…? • What facts or ideas show…? • What do the facts mean? • How is _____ related to _____? • Can you invent…? • Would it be better if…?	• move • match	• select • choose	• act/act out
Level 3—Developing • increased comprehension • simple sentences	• How did _____ happen? • Which is your best answer? • What questions would you ask about…? • Why do you think…? • If you could _____, what would you do? • How would you prove…?	• name • label • tell/say	• list • categorize	• respond (with 1–2 words) • group
Level 4—Expanding • very good comprehension • some errors in speech	• How would you show…? • How would you summarize…? • What would result if…? • What is the relationship between…? • What is an alternative to…? • Why is this important?	• recall • compare/ contrast • describe	• retell • explain • role-play	• define • summarize • restate
Level 5—Bridging • comprehension comparable to native English speakers • speaks using complex sentences	• How would you describe…? • What is meant by…? • How would you use…? • What ideas justify…? • What is an original way to show…? • Why is it better that…?	• analyze • evaluate • create	• defend • justify • express	• complete • support

How to Use This Book

Teacher Lesson Plans

Each lesson is presented in a straightforward, step-by-step format so that teachers can easily implement it right away.

Differentiation Strategies are highlighted for quick reference.

Standards are aligned to grade-level content and English language learner needs.

Materials lists outline items needed for each lesson. If lessons call for slide show software, you might use *Microsoft Powerpoint®* or *Prezi®*. Additional resources are listed on page 167.

English Language Support suggestions offer ideas for adapting and customizing the lesson.

Anchor Activities extend the lesson and promote further investigation and practice for students who finish early.

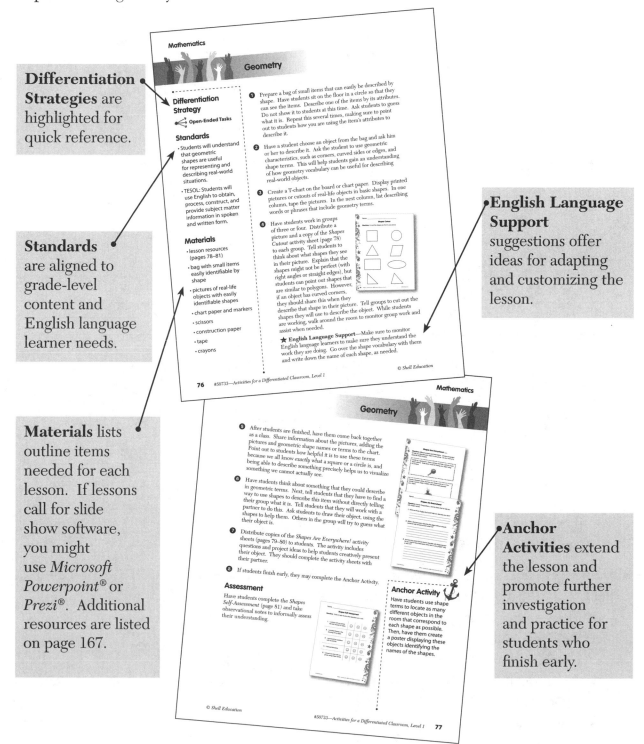

How to Use This Book *(cont.)*

Lesson Resources

These pages include student reproducibles and teacher resources needed to implement each lesson.

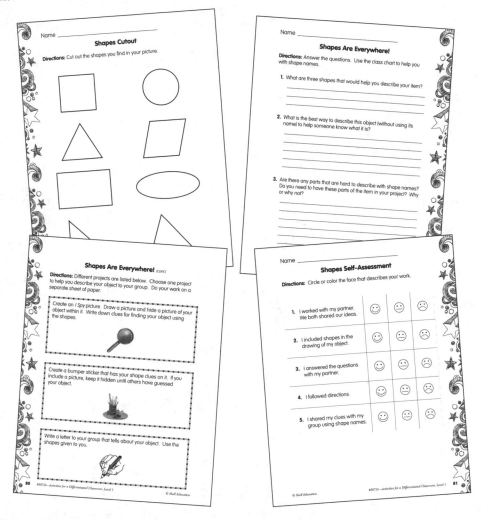

Teacher Resource CD

Helpful reproducibles and images are provided on the accompanying CD. Find a detailed listing of the CD contents on page 168.

- JPEGs of photographs
- Reproducible PDFs of all student activity sheets and teacher resource pages
- Reproducible PDFs of blank graphic organizers
- Answer key

Correlations to Standards

Shell Education is committed to producing educational materials that are research and standards based. In this effort, we have correlated all of our products to the academic standards of all 50 states, the District of Columbia, and the Department of Defense Dependent Schools.

How to Find Standards Correlations

To print a customized correlation report of this product for your state, visit our website at **http://www.shelleducation.com** and follow the on-screen directions. If you require assistance in printing correlation reports, please contact Customer Service at 1-877-777-3450.

Purpose and Intent of Standards

The No Child Left Behind (NCLB) legislation mandates that all states adopt academic standards that identify the skills students will learn in kindergarten through grade 12. While many states had already adopted academic standards prior to NCLB, the legislation set requirements to ensure the standards were detailed and comprehensive.

Standards are designed to focus instruction and guide adoption of curricula. Standards are statements that describe the criteria necessary for students to meet specific academic goals. They define the knowledge, skills, and content students should acquire at each level. Standards are also used to develop standardized tests to evaluate students' academic progress.

Teachers are required to demonstrate how their lessons meet state standards. State standards are used in the development of all of our products, so educators can be assured that they meet the academic requirements of each state.

McREL Compendium

We use the Mid-continent Research for Education and Learning (McREL) Compendium to create standards correlations. Each year, McREL analyzes state standards and revises the compendium. By following this procedure, McREL is able to produce a general compilation of national standards. Each lesson in this product is based on one or more McREL standards. The chart on page 20 lists each standard taught in this book and the page numbers for the corresponding lessons.

TESOL Standards

The lessons in this book promote English language development for English language learners. The standards listed on page 21, from the Teachers of English to Speakers of Other Languages (TESOL) Association, support the language objectives presented throughout the lessons.

Name _____

Memory Time Line

Directions: Think about the memory you shared with a friend. Answer the questions to help you think through your writing.

1. What is your favorite part of your memory?

   _____

   _____

   _____

2. Put your memory in order on a time line like the one below. Draw your time line on the back of this sheet.

   First   **Second**   **Third**   **Fourth**
   ●————————————————●————————————————●————————————————●

3. What words will be important to include in your story?

   _____

   _____

   _____

4. Imagine that you are experiencing your memory again. What would you see, hear, smell, feel, and think?

   Sights: _____

   Sounds: _____

   Smells: _____

   Feelings: _____

   Thoughts: _____

© Shell Education

Name _____

Memory Time Line

Directions: Think about the memory you shared with a friend. Answer the questions to help you think through your writing.

1. Why is this memory important to you?

   _____

   _____

   _____

2. Put your memory in order on a time line like the one below. Draw your time line on the back of this sheet.

   First   **Second**   **Third**   **Fourth**

3. What is your favorite part of your memory?

   _____

   _____

   _____

4. Add two or three sensory details about the most important part of your memory.

   _____

   _____

   _____

   _____

Name _____

Memory Time Line

Directions: Draw a picture that shows the most important part of your memory. Answer the questions to help you think about your writing.

Draw your picture here:

1. What happened first?

   _____

   _____

2. What happened second?

   _____

   _____

3. What happened third?

   _____

   _____

4. What happened fourth?

   _____

   _____

5. What is your favorite part of your memory?

   _____

   _____

Name _____

Class Memories Anchor Activity

Directions: Write a memory about one class picture. Answer the questions and follow the steps below.

1. What is the most important part of this memory?

   _____

   _____

   _____

2. Create a time line about the most important part of the memory. Draw your time line on the back of this sheet.

   First   **Second**   **Third**   **Fourth**

   ●━━━━━━━━━━━━━●━━━━━━━━━━━━━●━━━━━━━━━━━━━●

3. What words will you use to tell about what you were thinking and feeling?

   _____

   _____

   _____

   _____

4. What details should be part of your story?

   _____

   _____

   _____

5. Write your story on another sheet of paper.

Words Are Everywhere

Differentiation Strategy

 Leveled Learning Centers

Standards

- Students will understand level-appropriate sight words and vocabulary.

- TESOL: Students will use English to obtain, process, construct, and provide subject matter information in spoken and written form.

Materials

- lesson resources (pages 30–33)

- materials for centers (See Preparation Note.)

- index cards

- plastic storage bags

Preparation Note: Set up three centers in the classroom. Each center will offer different activities for students working at different readiness levels. Place the following materials at the specified center:

Center 1—Copies of the *Making Words* activity sheet (page 30); letter tiles, such as Scrabble® tiles

Center 2—Copies of the *Stamp Out Your Words* activity sheet (page 31); letter stamps; stamp pads

Center 3—Copies of the *Magazines and Words* activity sheet (page 32); magazines; scissors; craft sticks; glue

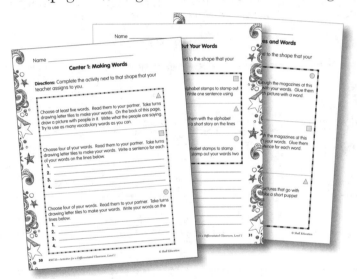

1 Create a classroom word wall of sight words and vocabulary words at varying levels of difficulty. Have students create personal dictionaries that are based on their reading level or word banks to use as they acquire new sight words and vocabulary in their reading and writing.

2 As students are learning words, have them write each new word on an index card. Have a plastic storage bag attached to their notebook or placed inside their work folder. Instruct students to keep their index cards in their plastic storage bag. This can be done throughout the year to help students learn new words.

★ **English Language Support**—Have English language learners write each word and then draw a picture of it to help them remember the meaning of the word.

Words Are Everywhere

❸ Partner students who have similar words to learn. As a whole class, model how to play *Go Fish* with the words. This is a simple activity to help students build fluency in a fun and engaging way.

- With their partners, students choose 10 to 15 words. Each student should use the same word cards.

- Each student chooses five cards without looking and leaves the rest of the cards in a stack facedown.

- Students try to make pairs of matching words by asking their partners for the match of a word they have in their hands.

- The partner either hands the student the card or says "Go fish" if he or she does not have the requested card. If the partner gives the card to the student, the student places both cards in a pile to the side.

❹ Tell students that as readers they are developing a larger vocabulary every day. Explain that in order to continue to grow as readers, they need to practice new words to help them build fluency in reading. For the lesson, students will need their sight word/vocabulary cards.

❺ Tell students that they will be given the choice of working in any of the three centers. Explain the centers and assign students a shape based on their readiness level.

❻ If students finish early, they may complete the Anchor Activity.

Assessment

Distribute the *Words Are Everywhere Self-Assessment* (page 33). Read the directions and each statement aloud to students, and allow them time to complete the reflection on their experience. This will provide one way to assess students' placement at different levels.

Activity Levels
▲
Above Grade Level
■
On Grade Level
●
Below Grade Level

Anchor Activity ⚓

Have students choose five new vocabulary words to challenge themselves in reading and writing. Encourage students to choose words from science lessons or another area of interest. Have them write each word, learn its meaning, and draw a picture to help them remember the meaning. They must also create movements for their words and teach other students the new words through a game of charades.

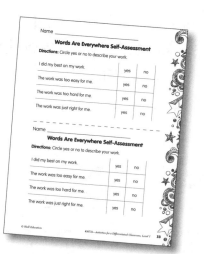

Name _____

Center 1: Making Words

Directions: Complete the activity next to the shape that your teacher assigns to you.

△

Choose at least five words. Read them to your partner. Take turns drawing letter tiles to make your words. On the back of this page, draw a picture with people in it. Write what the people are saying. Try to use as many vocabulary words as you can.

▢

Choose four of your words. Read them to your partner. Take turns drawing letter tiles to make your words. Write a sentence for each of your words on the lines below or in your journal.

1. _____
2. _____
3. _____
4. _____

◯

Choose four of your words. Read them to your partner. Take turns drawing letter tiles to make your words. Write your words on the lines below or in your journal.

1. _____
2. _____
3. _____
4. _____

Name _____

Center 2: Stamp Out Your Words

Directions: Complete the activity next to the shape that your teacher assigns to you.

□

Choose five of your words. Use the alphabet stamps to stamp out your words on the back of this sheet. Write one sentence using each word on the lines below.

△

Choose at least five words and stamp them with the alphabet stamps on the back of this sheet. Write a short story on the lines below using these words.

○

Choose four of your words. Use the alphabet stamps to stamp these words. On the back of this sheet, stamp out your words two times each.

_____

_____

_____

_____

_____

_____

Name _____

Center 3: Magazines and Words

Directions: Complete the activity next to the shape that your teacher assigns to you.

Choose three of your words. Look through the magazines at this center. Cut out three pictures that go with your words. Glue them on the back of this page and label each picture with a word.

Choose four of your words. Look through the magazines at this center. Cut out four pictures that go with your words. Glue them on the back of this page and write a sentence for each word.

Choose at least four words. Cut out four pictures that go with your words. Glue them on craft sticks. Make a short puppet show using these pictures and your words.

Name _____

Words Are Everywhere Self-Assessment

Directions: Circle yes or no to describe your work.

I did my best on my work.	yes	no
The work was too easy for me.	yes	no
The work was too hard for me.	yes	no
The work was just right for me.	yes	no

– –

Name _____

Words Are Everywhere Self-Assessment

Directions: Circle yes or no to describe your work.

I did my best on my work.	yes	no
The work was too easy for me.	yes	no
The work was too hard for me.	yes	no
The work was just right for me.	yes	no

Retelling

Differentiation Strategy

Multiple Intelligences

Standards

- Students will summarize information found in texts, for example, retell information in their own words.

- TESOL: Students will use English to obtain, process, construct, and provide subject matter information in spoken and written form.

Materials

- lesson resources (pages 36–39)

- children's books at various levels *(See page 167.)*

- index cards

- markers

- examples of time lines

- large construction paper

❶ Tell students that readers need to be able to summarize or retell events from a story in their own words. There are many reasons why readers need to be able to do this. Share real-life examples, such as retelling what you read to share information with others or retelling so that you understand something better and can use the information to help you. Share with students that retelling includes identifying the main characters in a story and the important events.

❷ Read a children's book that has a clear sequence of events. As you read, share your thinking aloud. Show students how to retell by thinking back through the story and flipping through the pictures. As you are modeling your thinking, list important events on index cards with a marker. Make the index cards visible to students. Model going back through the story to think about the events that happened, pointing out that good readers frequently reread. Tell students that rereading is an important strategy to help us remember and comprehend more about a story.

❸ Place the index cards with the listed story events in chronological order. Make sure to point out that you wrote these in your own words and the sentences did not come straight from the book. Next, model for your students how to decide which events are more important than others. Point out that if these events did not happen, the story would change.

❹ Pair students homogeneously for the following activities. Explain to students that they are going to be given a book to read with their partner. They will need to use the strategy that you modeled to identify the most important parts of the story to include in their retelling. Students will work together to create a retelling by doing one of the assigned activities: a skit (bodily/kinesthetic), a time line (logical/mathematical), or a poster advertisement (visual/spatial) to share with the class.

5 Choose which activity sheet students will complete based on the intelligence on which you want them to focus. Distribute copies of the selected *Readers Retell* activity sheets (pages 36–38) to students. (Have time line examples available for students completing the *Readers Retell Time Line* activity sheet on page 37.)

★ **English Language Support**—When English language learners are done reading, ask them to retell the story to you, using the pictures in the book, before they create a product that includes their retelling. This will help them think through their summary before they make decisions about the final retelling.

6 If students finish early, they may complete the Anchor Activity.

Assessment

To keep track of students' understanding, fill out the *Readers Retell Assessment Checklist* (page 39). Keep this in a portfolio and refer back to it periodically to make sure that students are progressing throughout the year.

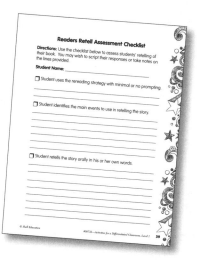

Anchor Activity

Have students choose a picture book to retell. Have them take on the role of the main character. They should write the retelling of the story (using the previously discussed strategies) and be prepared to retell this story in front of the class, pretending to be the character from the book.

Name _____

Readers Retell Skit

Directions: Read the book with your partner. Think about the most important parts in the story. Use the space below to retell the story with pictures.

Use this space to retell the story in your own words.

_____

_____

_____

_____

_____

_____

_____ .

Perform a skit to retell this story to the class. Remember to include characters and the important parts.

Name _____

Readers Retell Time Line

Directions: Read the book with your partner. Think about the most important parts in the story. Use the space below to retell the story with pictures.

Use this space to retell the story in your own words.

_____

_____

_____

_____

_____

_____

_____

On the back of this sheet, make a time line that shows the main characters and the important events in order. You will need to record five events.

Name _____

Readers Retell Poster

Directions: Read the book with your partner. Think about the most important parts in the story. Use the space below to retell the story with pictures.

Use this space to retell the story in your own words.

_____

_____

_____

_____

_____

_____

Make a poster for this book on a large sheet of paper. Make sure it has the main characters and the important events on it.

Readers Retell Assessment Checklist

Directions: Use the checklist below to assess students' retelling of their book. You may wish to script their responses or take notes on the lines provided.

Student Name: _____

☐ Student uses the rereading strategy with minimal or no prompting.

_____

_____

☐ Student identifies the main events to use in retelling the story.

_____

_____

_____

_____

_____

☐ Student retells the story orally in his or her own words.

_____

_____

_____

_____

_____

_____

_____

Reading for Fluency

Differentiation Strategy

Tiered Assignments

Standards

• Students will read aloud familiar stories, poems, and passages with fluency and expression.

• TESOL: Students will use English to obtain, process, construct, and provide subject matter information in spoken and written form.

Materials

• lesson resources (pages 42–45)

• independent reading materials for each student *(See page 167.)*

• chart paper and markers

• audio recordings of books

• listening center materials

• vocabulary picture cards

• sight words list (sightwords.pdf)

Preparation Note: Be sure that your students have books that are at their instructional level for this activity.

1 Tell students that fluency is an important part of reading. Fluent readers are able to read text accurately and with ease. Fluency allows readers to understand more of what they are reading, which helps them to remember more about the text.

2 Model reading a book without fluency—stopping and struggling with words, reading very slowly, and skipping or rearranging words so that it does not make sense. Ask your students what they noticed about your reading. Make a T-chart on chart paper to list what nonfluent reading sounds like and what fluent reading sounds like. Model reading a book with fluency—reading at an appropriate pace, accurately, and with expression—and ask students what they noticed. Add this to the chart.

3 Distribute instructional-level books to students. Tell students that they are going to work toward being fluent readers. Distribute copies of the *Reading Fluently* activity sheets (pages 42–44) to students based on their readiness levels. Make sure below-grade-level students have access to a word wall or list of sight words for practice.

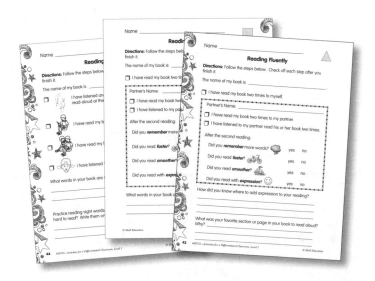

Reading for Fluency

4 Explain the directions and remind students that the purpose of this practice is to read with fewer errors, at a smoother pace, and with expression.

★ **English Language Support**—Partner English language learners with language-proficient students who are close in reading level and have them listen to their texts *first* at the listening center. Make sure English language learners have vocabulary picture cards that go along with the text they are reading.

5 If students finish early, they may complete the Anchor Activity.

Activity Levels
▲
Above Grade Level
■
On Grade Level
●
Below Grade Level

Assessment

Meet with all students individually. Listen to them read, provide specific feedback, and take anecdotal notes about their performance. You may wish to document the *accuracy* with which students decode words, their *automaticity*, or ability to decode words automatically (without sounding out), and their *prosody*, or vocal expression. Use the *Fluency Growth Assessment* (page 45) to track each student's progress towards fluency. (You will need one assessment sheet for each student.)

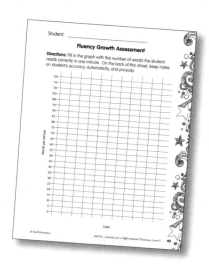

Anchor Activity

Have students choose a poem (either on their own or with a partner) to prepare and present to the class. Provide poetry books or copies of poems for students to read. They should practice reading the poem many times to ensure that they are able to read it fluently for their classmates.

Name _____

Reading Fluently

Directions: Follow the steps below. Check off each step after you finish it.

The name of my book is _____ .

☐ I have read my book two times to myself.

Partner's Name: _____

☐ I have read my book two times to my partner.

☐ I have listened to my partner read his or her book two times.

After the second reading:

Did you **remember** more words?   yes   no

Did you read **faster**?   yes   no

Did you read **smoother**?   yes   no

Did you read with **expression**?   yes   no

How did you know where to add expression to your reading?

_____

_____

_____

What was your favorite section or page in your book to read aloud? Why? _____

_____

_____

Name _____

Reading Fluently

Directions: Follow the steps below. Check off each step after you finish it.

The name of my book is _____ .

☐ I have read my book two times to myself.

Partner's Name: _____

☐ I have read my book two times to my partner.

☐ I have listened to my partner read his or her book two times.

After the second reading:

Did you **remember** more words?   yes   no

Did you read **faster**?   yes   no

Did you read **smoother**?   yes   no

Did you read with **expression**?   yes   no

What words in your book are still hard to read?

_____   _____

_____   _____

Name _____

Reading Fluently

Directions: Follow the steps below. Check off each step after you finish it.

The name of my book is _____ .

☐   I have listened and followed along with the book read-aloud at the listening center.

☐   I have read my book two times to myself.

☐   I have read my book to my partner.

☐   I have listened to my partner read his or her book.

What words in your book are still hard to read?

_____   _____

_____   _____

Practice reading sight words to your partner. Which sight words are hard to read? Write them on the lines below.

_____   _____

_____   _____

Student: _____

Fluency Growth Assessment

Directions: Fill in the graph with the number of words the student reads correctly in one minute. On the back of this sheet, keep notes on student's accuracy, automaticity, and prosody.

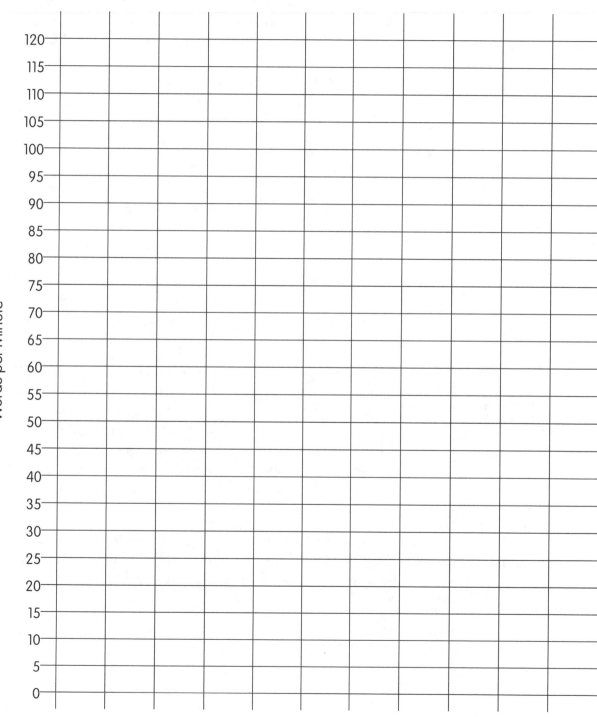

Date

Poetry

Differentiation Strategy

 Open-Ended Tasks

Standards

- Students will write in a variety of forms or genres such as poems.

- TESOL: Students will use English to obtain, process, construct, and provide subject matter information in spoken and written form.

Materials

- lesson resources (pages 48–51)

- copies of several poems (*See page 167.*)

- chart paper and markers

- construction paper

- crayons or markers

- photographs

- CD of nature recordings (*optional*)

❶ Share several short poems that are appropriate for children. After reading these with students, ask them to brainstorm what they see or notice about poetry. Give students time to talk with partners and then make a class chart that lists their observations. They might make observations such as poems are short and long, they do not always have punctuation, or they make them feel happy or sad. Discuss and clarify students' comments as they are added to the class chart.

❷ Let students choose one of the poems that was shared in Step 1. Distribute copies of the poems and have students read their poem aloud to a partner several times. Ask students what they are thinking about when they are reading the poem and have them share with their partners. Listen to determine whether students are talking about visualizing the poem.

❸ Have students copy their poem onto construction paper. Tell students that poets want readers to imagine what they have written about. Have students draw what they imagined while they were reading the poem.

❹ Explain that poets strive to create a picture in a reader's mind by using *adjectives*, or describing words, in their poems. Take a nature walk or play a CD with nature sounds. Have students brainstorm a list of adjectives to describe the sounds they hear. Show photographs to your students and have them brainstorm describing words for these photos. Post the student-generated list of adjectives in a visible place to help students with their writing.

❺ Tell students that they are going to write their own poems. They should include describing words to help readers get a picture in their mind. They should also write a poem about something they care about.

6 Distribute copies of the *Poetry Prewriting* activity sheet (page 48) to students. Have students answer the questions before drafting their poems.

★ **English Language Support**—Clarify directions with English language learners. Review the list of adjectives created by the class and encourage them to use the list as a resource for words in their poems.

7 Distribute copies of the *Poetry Writing* activity sheet (page 49) to students. Once students are finished writing their poems, they should choose a way to share one with an audience. Students can act it out, read it, or create a poster of their poem and illustrations.

8 If students finish early, they may complete the Anchor Activity.

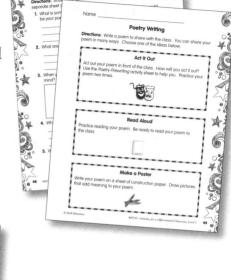

Assessment

Use the *Poetry Assessment* (page 50) to record students' performance on this writing project. Conference with students about their poems, asking questions such as: Why did you choose this topic? What describing words did you include?

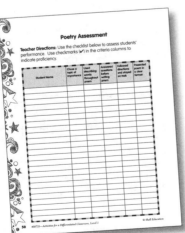

Anchor Activity

Have students read through poetry books, choosing as many poems as they would like to include in an anthology. Distribute copies of the *Poetry Anchor Activity* activity sheet (page 51) to students. Make booklets in advance by stapling drawing paper together. Have students write the title and author of their favorite poems and include illustrations of these poems.

Name _____

Poetry Prewriting

Directions: Answer the questions below. Then, write your poem on a separate sheet of paper.

1. What is something that you are excited about? Why? This could be your poem's topic.

   _____
   _____
   _____

2. What are some words that describe your topic?

   _____
   _____
   _____

3. When you think about your topic, what pictures come to your mind? Draw one of these pictures.

   ```
   ┌─────────────────────────────────────┐
   │                                     │
   │                                     │
   │                                     │
   │                                     │
   │                                     │
   └─────────────────────────────────────┘
   ```

4. What sound words can you include in your poem?

   _____
   _____
   _____

5. What do you want to say about this topic?

   _____
   _____
   _____

Name _____

Poetry Writing

Directions: Write a poem to share with the class. You can share your poem in many ways. Choose one of the ideas below.

Act It Out

Act out your poem in front of the class. How will you act it out? Use the *Poetry Prewriting* activity sheet to help you. Practice your poem two times.

Read Aloud

Practice reading your poem. Be ready to read your poem to the class.

Make a Poster

Write your poem on a sheet of construction paper. Draw pictures that add meaning to your poem.

Poetry Assessment

Teacher Directions: Use the checklist below to assess students' performance. Use checkmarks (✔) in the criteria columns to indicate proficiency.

Student Name	Chose a topic of importance	Used describing words throughout poem	Answered questions before writing poem	Followed directions and stayed on task	Presented poem in a clear format

Name _____

Poetry Anchor Activity

Directions: Read the poetry books. Choose some poems to make your own poetry book. Use the materials your teacher gave you to make a book.

Write down the poem's title and the poet's name.

Draw a picture to go with each poem.

Only one poem should go on each page.

Look at the example below:

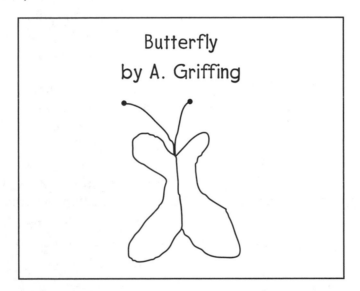

Why do you like the poems you chose? Be ready to share your reasons with the class.

_____

_____

_____

_____

_____

_____

_____

Descriptive Words

Differentiation Strategy

 Menu of Options

Standards

- Students will understand and use descriptive words to convey basic ideas.

- TESOL: Students will use English to obtain, process, construct, and provide subject matter information in spoken and written form.

Materials

- lesson resources (pages 54–57)
- photographs
- index cards
- timer
- chart paper and markers
- adjectives word bank
- art supplies, puppets

Preparation Note: Gather enough interesting photographs for each student to have one.

1 Share an interesting photograph with the whole class. Model how to brainstorm descriptive words for this picture.

2 Tell students that a writer not only needs to think about what the picture looks like but also what things in the picture might smell like, sound like, taste like, and how people might be feeling. Tell students that it can be boring when a writer uses words like *big* or *good*. Instead, a writer should strive to use just the right word to describe something so a reader can really picture it, and also so it is interesting. For example, they might replace *the good snack* with *the delicious apple*.

3 Tell students that they are going to do a picture pass. Explain that everyone will start with one picture. Ask students to look at the photograph and, on an index card, list as many descriptive words and action words (adjectives and verbs) as they can think of for the picture. When the timer goes off, they will pass their picture to the right and then they will work in silence again, listing as many words as possible for their new picture. Tell students that all of their words can go on one list. If students have difficulty with this task, pause between passes and share some examples as guidance.

4 After the picture pass, ask students to share their words with a partner. Then, as a whole class, have students share their descriptive words to create a class chart. List words only once and tell students that they will add to this chart throughout the school year with new words to help them improve their writing.

5 For independent practice, distribute copies of the *Descriptive Words for Holidays* activity sheet (page 54) to students. Read the directions to the class. Then, have students complete the activity sheet. Have volunteers share their descriptive words with the class. Write these words on the chart.

Descriptive Words

6 Distribute copies of the *Descriptive Words Menu of Options* activity sheet (page 55). Explain the directions to students and answer any questions that they might have. Pair students based on choices so that they will have a partner to work with throughout the project.

★ **English Language Support**—Pair English language learners with language-proficient students. Also, provide a word bank of adjectives for students to reference. This might be organized by synonyms for more basic words, such as *racing* and *jogging* for *run*.

7 If students finish early, they may complete the Anchor Activity.

Assessment

To assess students' understanding of the concept, complete the *Descriptive Words Rubric* (page 56).

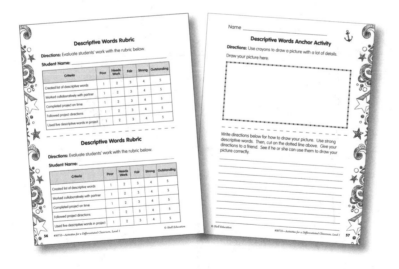

Anchor Activity ⚓

Have students draw a picture with many details using the *Descriptive Words Anchor Activity* activity sheet (page 57). Next, have them write directions on how to re-create their picture. They should use clear descriptive words to help others understand how to accurately draw the picture. Then, students can ask a friend to follow their directions for drawing the picture.

Name _____

Descriptive Words for Holidays

Directions: Think of your favorite holiday. What does it smell like? What does it sound like? What do you see, feel, and taste on that holiday? Use the body below. Write two descriptive words about this holiday for each of your senses.

Holiday: _____

_____

_____   _____

_____

_____   _____

_____   _____

_____

_____

Name _____

Descriptive Words Menu of Options

Directions: Choose one activity from the box below to practice using descriptive words in your writing.

Activity Choices

1. Create a travel brochure about your favorite place to go. Tell about your favorite place. Use at least five descriptive words.

2. Make a poster that describes the classroom. Make sure you include at least five descriptive words.

3. Perform a puppet show with two puppets. Use at least five descriptive words in your puppet show.

4. Write a story. Use at least five descriptive words in your story.

5. Think about your favorite snack. Write about this favorite snack. Use at least five descriptive words.

Descriptive Words Rubric

Directions: Evaluate students' work with the rubric below.

Student Name: _____

Criteria	Poor	Needs Work	Fair	Strong	Outstanding
Created list of descriptive words	1	2	3	4	5
Worked collaboratively with partner	1	2	3	4	5
Completed project on time	1	2	3	4	5
Followed project directions	1	2	3	4	5
Used five descriptive words in project	1	2	3	4	5

- -

Descriptive Words Rubric

Directions: Evaluate students' work with the rubric below.

Student Name: _____

Criteria	Poor	Needs Work	Fair	Strong	Outstanding
Created list of descriptive words	1	2	3	4	5
Worked collaboratively with partner	1	2	3	4	5
Completed project on time	1	2	3	4	5
Followed project directions	1	2	3	4	5
Used five descriptive words in project	1	2	3	4	5

Name _____

Descriptive Words Anchor Activity

Directions: Use crayons to draw a picture with a lot of details.

Draw your picture here:

- -

Write directions below for how to draw your picture. Use strong descriptive words. Then, cut on the dotted line above. Give your directions to a friend. See if he or she can use them to draw your picture correctly.

_____

_____

_____

_____

_____

_____

_____

_____

_____

More-or-Less Story Problems

Differentiation Strategy

 Leveled Learning Centers

Standards

• Students will add and subtract whole numbers.

• TESOL: Students will use English to obtain, process, construct, and provide subject matter information in spoken and written form.

Materials

• lesson resources (pages 60–63)

• stamps and stamp pads

• counters

• construction paper

• large chart paper

• clipboards (optional)

Preparation Note: Set up three centers around the classroom. Place the following items at the specified center:

Center 1—Copies of the *Stamp Out Math Problems* activity sheet (page 60); stamps; stamp pads

Center 2—Copies of the *Number Line* activity sheet (page 61)

Center 3—Copies of the *Picture the Math* activity sheet (page 62); counters

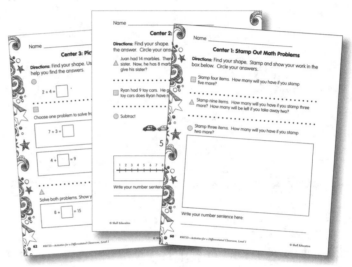

1 Model the math concepts of joining and taking away. Provide the following scenario: Two boys are working together (have two boys come up to the front of the room). Then, six girls join them (have six girls come up to the front of the room). Ask the class how many students there are all together. Continue to demonstrate a few more problems this way.

2 Pair students with partners. Distribute counters and construction paper to students. Provide a story problem to the whole group but change the numbers in the story problem to fit your students' needs. A story problem example could be: *Matt has seven pretzels, then his sister gives him five more. How many pretzels does he have now?* Point out phrases such as *five more* and *how many now?* and explain their meaning. Make sure English language learners understand the vocabulary. Give partners time to work through problems, using counters or a different strategy that works for them.

More-or-Less Story Problems

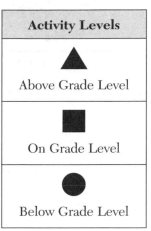

Activity Levels

▲
Above Grade Level
■
On Grade Level
●
Below Grade Level

❸ Allow students to share how they solved this problem. Focus on what strategies are discussed and create a chart with problem-solving strategies listed on it. Such strategies might include drawing a picture, using a number line, using a hundred chart, using objects, or writing a number sentence.

❹ Model the strategy of drawing a picture. Give students this example: *Six pencils were on Sara's desk this morning. Then Andy gave her four more. How many pencils does Sara have in all?* Draw this step-by-step to demonstrate the strategy.

❺ Model using a number line for the problem in Step 4 to show students how different strategies can lead to the same answer.

❻ Tell students that they will rotate through three centers. Assign students a shape that corresponds to their readiness levels. Tell them that they will complete the activity at each center that has that same shape.

❼ Explain the centers. Assign students to the centers. Have students use clipboards if there is not enough table or desk space to write at the centers.

❽ Allow students time to work at a center. Then, have the students rotate to a new center.

★ **English Language Support**—Give English language learners appropriate tasks based on their abilities and make sure to place them in centers with language-proficient students. Be at hand to assist these students as they work.

❾ If students finish work early in a center, they can begin the Anchor Activity while they wait to rotate.

Assessment

Circulate as students work at centers and ask students questions to determine their levels of understanding. Take anecdotal notes to keep with students' records.

Anchor Activity

Have students use the *My Own Math Story Problem Anchor Activity* activity sheet (page 63) to create a book of math story problems that can be shared with other students. They will write as many problems as time allows, and they must also create an answer key to show their thinking and strategies used to solve the problem. They can then trade problems with others, working to solve one another's problems.

Name _____

Center 1: Stamp Out Math Problems

Directions: Find your shape. Stamp and show your work in the box below. Circle your answers.

☐ Stamp four items. How many will you have if you stamp five more?

• •

△ Stamp nine items. How many will you have if you stamp three more? How many will be left if you take away two?

• •

⚪ Stamp three items. How many will you have if you stamp two more?

Write your number sentence here:

_____

Name _____

Center 2: Number Line

Directions: Find your shape. Use the number line below to find the answer. Circle your answer on the number line.

 Juan had 14 marbles. Then, he shared some marbles with his sister. Now, he has 8 marbles left. How many marbles did Juan give his sister?

• •

☐ Ryan had 9 toy cars. He gave 5 cars to his brother. How many toy cars does Ryan have now?

• •

◯ Subtract

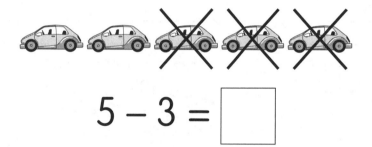

$$5 - 3 = \boxed{}$$

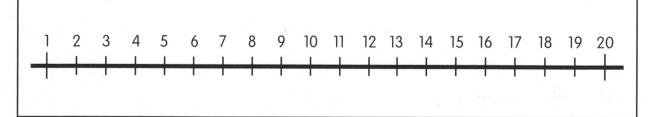

Write your number sentence here:

_____

Name _____

Center 3: Picture the Math

Directions: Find your shape. Use counters and draw pictures to help you find the answers.

$2 + 4 =$ ☐ $6 - 3 =$ ☐

∙ ∙

☐

Choose one problem to solve from each box. Show your work.

$7 + 3 =$ ☐ $8 - 4 =$ ☐

$4 +$ ☐ $= 9$ $10 -$ ☐ $= 6$

∙ ∙

△

Solve both problems. Show your work.

$8 +$ ☐ $= 15$ ☐ $- 4 = 9$

Name _____

My Own Math Story Problem Anchor Activity

Directions: Write your own math story problem below. Then, make an answer page. Cut out both boxes to be placed in a class book.

Write your math story problem in the box below.

Name _____

Math Story Problem

_____

_____

_____

_____

_____

_____

Use drawings to show your work and the answer in the box below.

Name _____

Math Story Problem Answer

Fractions!

Differentiation Objective

 Multiple Intelligences

Standards

- Students will understand the concept of a unit and its subdivision into equal parts.
- TESOL: Students will use English to obtain, process, construct, and provide subject matter information in spoken and written form.

Materials

- lesson resources (pages 66–69)
- construction paper
- chart paper and markers
- snap cubes
- paper bags
- math journals
- CD or MP3 player

1 Partner students heterogeneously. Distribute one construction-paper square to each pair and tell students to pretend the square is a brownie. Tell students that you need them to share this brownie equally among one another. Ask the question: How will you do that? Give partners time to talk and share out their different strategies. List ideas on a class chart.

2 Distribute bags filled with 20 snap cubes in a variety of colors to groups of four students.

★ **English Language Support**—Be sure to model the next several steps for your English language learners. Give the instructions for students to pull out the cubes and then repeat the instructions while modeling the action.

3 Have each member of the group pull out four different cubes (without looking) and link them together. Tell students to draw their snap cubes (linked together) in their math journals and record how many of each color they have out of four (for example, *3 out of 4 are yellow cubes*). Have students share the information with the members of their group.

4 Explain to students that they are going to carry their snap cubes linked together and move to music. Have students walk around the room until the music stops and then find a partner. They should share with one another how many cubes of each color they have out of four. Walk around, listening to students as they share their thinking.

5 After several rounds, have students return to their seats. Ask students to make half of their four cubes one color and half another color. Ask students the following question: How do you know that two equal amounts makes two halves? Give students time to talk in their groups. They should respond or can be prompted that they counted the cubes to make the same amount (two) of each color. Point out that *equal* means the same amount.

6 Have groups return all but eight of the cubes to the bag. Ask students to show you how they would share these cubes equally among themselves. Move around the room and listen to the discussions about this task. Ask students to explain what they did as a group to make sure they shared all of their cubes equally. Ask students to put away two cubes so that there are only six cubes for four people. Prompt students to think about what they would do to share the six cubes among four people and allow students time to talk. They will not be able to halve the cubes, but they should be able to verbalize this. Again, have students share their thoughts, adding strategies and ideas to the class chart that was started in Step 1.

7 Display the *Candy to Share: Story* activity sheet (page 66), the *Candy to Share: Picture* activity sheet (page 67), and the *Candy to Share: Play* activity sheet (page 68) and explain the activities to students. Have students choose a partner to work with, and allow them to choose which activity sheet they would like to complete.

★ **English Language Support**—Meet with your English language learners in a small group and explain the directions, using actions and gestures. Depending on their writing abilities, make adjustments for the written part of the activity, allowing them to explain answers orally instead of writing them.

8 If students finish early, they may complete the Anchor Activity.

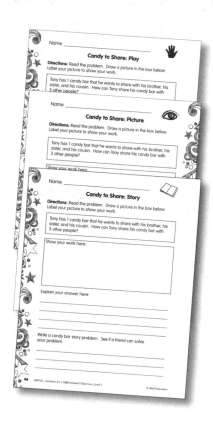

Anchor Activity

Have students decorate a bulletin board with real-life fractions. Drawings, photos, or other items that can be broken apart into fractions can be labeled and added to the bulletin board.

Assessment

Use the *Fractions Self-Assessment* (page 69) to assess students' understanding of problem solving with fractions. Look closely at their thinking on number 6. Are they able to explain their thinking? Are they able to show their thinking with pictures? Do they need more support with this concept? Do they need different (less abstract) models or representations to help them with this concept? Use the responses to guide instruction for each student.

Name _____

Candy to Share: Story

Directions: Read the problem. Draw a picture in the box below.
Label your picture to show your work.

Tony has 1 candy bar that he wants to share with his brother, his
sister, and his cousin. How can Tony share his candy bar with
3 other people?

Show your work here:

Explain your answer here:

_____

_____

_____

Write a candy bar story problem. See if a friend can solve
your problem.

_____

_____

_____

 #50733—*Activities for a Differentiated Classroom, Level 1*

Name _____

Candy to Share: Picture

Directions: Read the problem. Draw a picture in the box below.
Label your picture to show your work.

> Tony has 1 candy bar that he wants to share with his brother, his
> sister, and his cousin. How can Tony share his candy bar with
> 3 other people?

Show your work here:

Explain your answer here:

_____

_____

_____

Draw a picture that shows another candy bar sharing problem here:

Name _____

Candy to Share: Play

Directions: Read the problem. Draw a picture in the box below.
Label your picture to show your work.

Tony has 1 candy bar that he wants to share with his brother, his
sister, and his cousin. How can Tony share his candy bar with
3 other people?

Show your work here:

Explain your answer here:

_____

_____

_____

_____

_____

_____

Create a play that includes the candy bar problem. Act out how to
solve this problem.

Name _____

Fractions Self-Assessment

Directions: Circle or color the face that describes your work.

1. I worked with my partner to solve this problem.

2. I showed my thinking with this problem.

3. I wrote down how I solved this problem with words.

4. I followed the directions for my activity.

5. I understand how to share a candy bar with four people.

6. I know how to share 6 pieces of a candy bar with 4 people.

Explain how to share 6 pieces of a candy bar with 4 people. Show your work with words and pictures below.

Measurement

Differentiation Objective

Three-Story Intellect

Standards

- Students will make quantitative estimates of familiar linear dimensions and check them against measurements.

- TESOL: Students will use English to obtain, process, construct, and provide subject matter information in spoken and written form.

Materials

- lesson resources (pages 72–75)

- paper clips or other small items

- index cards

❶ Ask students the following questions: How do you know if something is bigger than something else? What does bigger mean? What are the different ways something can be bigger than something else? Let students brainstorm and share with a partner or in a small group. Share ideas as a whole class.

❷ Model how to measure length using a nonstandard unit of measure, such as hands or feet. Have students practice measuring things in the classroom and discuss measurements as a class. Walk around while students are measuring and clarify any misunderstandings they may have.

❸ Measure an object in the classroom, such as a bookshelf. Using that measurement (e.g., 10 first-grader hands for a bookshelf), ask students to compare a student standing next to the bookshelf. Ask them, "Is he taller or shorter than the bookshelf? If we measure him, do you think he is going to be more than or less than 10 hands?" Ask students to record a guess for the student's height (in hands) on scratch paper. Tell students that this guess is called an *estimate*. Explain to students that we base our estimates on something we know. In this case, we made an estimate about the student's height by comparing him to the height of the bookshelf, which we know. Measure the student and discuss how close students' estimates were to the actual measurement. Emphasize that a good estimate is close to the actual measurement but is not expected to be exact.

❹ Continue to give examples of two objects close in size in the classroom, having students measure one and then make an estimate about the other. Encourage students to use the words *estimate* and *about*. While students are measuring and sharing, talk to the English language learners to check for understanding about the vocabulary and the concept of measurement. Ask them to explain to you what they have learned. Clarify any misconceptions at this time and provide math vocabulary terms on index cards with examples.

Measurement

5 Distribute copies of the *Measure Me!* activity sheets (pages 72–74) to students based on their readiness levels. Divide the class into homogeneous pairs, and have them work together in groups of four. Explain the directions and give students time to ask questions. Have students determine a nonstandard unit of measure to use, such as a hand or a book. Note that students with the circle activity sheets will need small items, such as paper clips, with which to measure illustrations.

These activities use the Three-Story Intellect Model to differentiate types of questions. The below-grade-level students will answer Level I and II questions.

Activity Levels
▲
Above Grade Level
■
On Grade Level
●
Below Grade Level

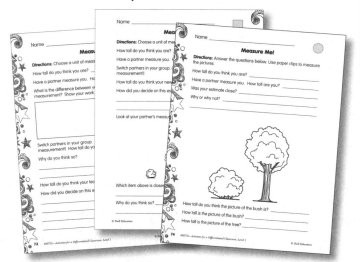

On-grade-level students will answer Level I, II, and III questions. Above-grade-level students will answer Level II and III questions.

★ **English Language Support**—Assign English language learners the appropriate tasks based on their readiness levels and make sure to pair them with language-proficient students.

6 If students finish early, they may complete the Anchor Activity.

Assessment

To assess students' understanding, have them respond to this question in writing: When you estimate how tall or long something is, what information do you use to help you make your estimate? Additional questions may include the following: If a laptop is 4 hands long, how long do you think your desk is? Why? Provide plenty of time for students to think through these questions and record their answers. Allow English language learners and struggling writers to explain their thinking orally.

Anchor Activity

Have students make a book titled "One Hand and Beyond." Distribute the *One Hand and Beyond Anchor Activity* activity sheet (page 75). In advance, prepare booklets of stapled sheets of blank paper. Have students follow the directions to complete the activity.

Name _____

Measure Me!

Directions: Choose a unit of measure. Answer the questions below.

How tall do you think you are? _____

Have a partner measure you. How tall are you? _____

What is the difference between your estimate and the actual measurement? Show your work below.

[ ]

Switch partners in your group. (Do not look at your new partner's measurement!) How tall do you think your new partner is? _____

Why do you think so?

_____

_____

How tall do you think your teacher is? _____

How did you decide on this estimate?

_____

_____

_____

_____

Name _____

Measure Me!

Directions: Choose a unit of measure. Answer the questions below.

How tall do you think you are? _____

Have a partner measure you. How tall are you? _____

Switch partners in your group. (Do not look at your new partner's measurement!)

How tall do you think your new partner is? _____

How did you decide on this estimate? _____

_____

_____

Look at your partner's measurement. Was your estimate close? ____

Which item above is closest to your height in real size?

_____

Why do you think so? _____

_____

Measure Me!

Directions: Answer the questions below. Use paper clips to measure the pictures.

How tall do you think you are? _____

Have a partner measure you. How tall are you? _____

Was your estimate close? _____

Why or why not? _____

_____

How tall do you think the picture of the bush is? _____

How tall is the picture of the bush? _____

How tall is the picture of the tree? _____

Name _____

One Hand and Beyond Anchor Activity

One Hand and Beyond

By: _____

Directions: Follow the steps below.

1. Write the title for your book: One Hand and Beyond.

2. Find something that measures about one hand.

3. Draw a picture of it on the first page of your book.

4. Label your picture *1 hand*.

5. Find things that are 2 hands, 3 hands, and 4 hands long. Draw pictures and label them to make more pages for your book.

6. Answer this question for each page: What else do you think is _____ hands tall or long? Why?

7. Make as many pages as you can. Color your pictures when you are done.

Geometry

Differentiation Strategy

Open-Ended Tasks

Standards

• Students will understand that geometric shapes are useful for representing and describing real-world situations.

• TESOL: Students will use English to obtain, process, construct, and provide subject matter information in spoken and written form.

Materials

• lesson resources (pages 78–81)

• bag with small items easily identifiable by shape

• pictures of real-life objects with easily identifiable shapes

• chart paper and markers

• scissors

• construction paper

• tape

• crayons

❶ Prepare a bag of small items that can easily be described by shape. Have students sit on the floor in a circle so that they can see the items. Describe one of the items by its attributes. Do not show it to students at this time. Ask students to guess what it is. Repeat this several times, making sure to point out to students how you are using the item's attributes to describe it.

❷ Have a student choose an object from the bag and ask him or her to describe it. Ask the student to use geometric characteristics, such as corners, curved sides or edges, and shape terms. This will help students gain an understanding of how geometry vocabulary can be useful for describing real-world objects.

❸ Create a T-chart on the board or chart paper. Display printed pictures or cutouts of real-life objects in basic shapes. In one column, tape the pictures. In the next column, list describing words or phrases that include geometry terms.

❹ Have students work in groups of three or four. Distribute a picture and a copy of the *Shapes Cutout* activity sheet (page 78) to each group. Tell students to think about what shapes they see in their picture. Explain that the shapes might not be perfect (with right angles or straight edges), but students can point out shapes that are similar to polygons. However, if an object has curved corners, they should share this when they describe that shape in their picture. Tell groups to cut out the shapes they will use to describe the object. While students are working, walk around the room to monitor group work and assist when needed.

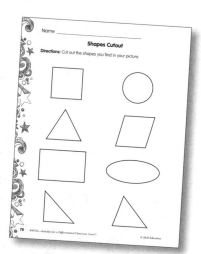

★ **English Language Support**—Make sure to monitor English language learners to make sure they understand the work they are doing. Go over the shape vocabulary with them and write down the name of each shape, as needed.

Geometry

5 After students are finished, have them come back together as a class. Share information about the pictures, adding the pictures and geometric shape names or terms to the chart. Point out to students how helpful it is to use these terms because we all know *exactly* what a square or a circle is, and being able to describe something precisely helps us to visualize something we cannot actually see.

6 Have students think about something that they could describe in geometric terms. Next, tell students that they have to find a way to use shapes to describe this item without directly telling their group what it is. Tell students that they will work with a partner to do this. Ask students to draw their object, using the shapes to help them. Others in the group will try to guess what their object is.

7 Distribute copies of the *Shapes Are Everywhere!* activity sheets (pages 79–80) to students. The activity includes questions and project ideas to help students creatively present their object. They should complete the activity sheets with their partner.

8 If students finish early, they may complete the Anchor Activity.

Assessment

Have students complete the *Shapes Self-Assessment* (page 81) and take observational notes to informally assess their understanding.

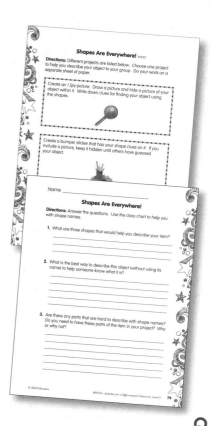

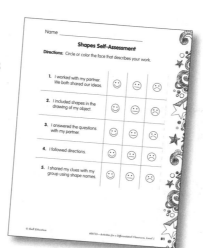

Anchor Activity

Have students use shape terms to locate as many different objects in the room that correspond to each shape as possible. Then, have them create a poster displaying these objects and identifying the names of the shapes.

Name  _____

Shapes Cutout

Directions: Cut out the shapes you find in your picture.

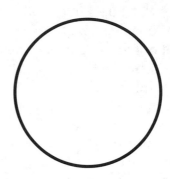

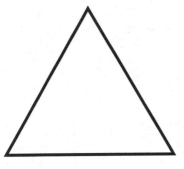

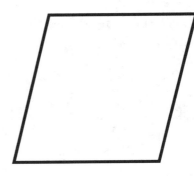

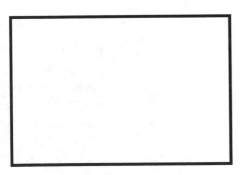

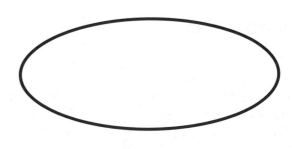

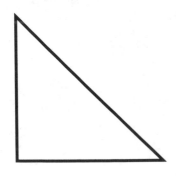

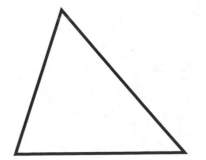

#50733—*Activities for a Differentiated Classroom, Level 1*   © *Shell Education*

Name _____

Shapes Are Everywhere!

Directions: Answer the questions. Use the class chart to help you with shape names.

1. What are three shapes that would help you describe your item?

_____

_____

_____

2. What is the best way to describe this object (without using its name) to help someone know what it is?

_____

_____

_____

_____

_____

3. Are there any parts that are hard to describe with shape names? Do you need to have these parts of the item in your project? Why or why not?

_____

_____

_____

_____

_____

Shapes Are Everywhere! *(cont.)*

Directions: Different projects are listed below. Choose one project to help you describe your object to your group. Do your work on a separate sheet of paper.

Create an *I Spy* picture. Draw a picture and hide a picture of your object within it. Write down clues for finding your object using the shapes.

Create a bumper sticker that has your shape clues on it. If you include a picture, keep it hidden until others have guessed your object.

Write a letter to your group that tells about your object. Use the shapes given to you.

Name _____

Shapes Self-Assessment

Directions: Circle or color the face that describes your work.

1. I worked with my partner. We both shared our ideas.	☺	😐	☹
2. I included shapes in the drawing of my object.	☺	😐	☹
3. I answered the questions with my partner.	☺	😐	☹
4. I followed directions.	☺	😐	☹
5. I shared my clues with my group using shape names.	☺	😐	☹

Extending Patterns

Differentiation Strategy

 Tiered Assignments

Standards

- Students will extend simple patterns.

- TESOL: Students will use English to obtain, process, construct, and provide subject matter information in spoken and written form.

Materials

- lesson resources (pages 84–87)
- chart paper and markers
- picture of a tricycle (tricycle.jpg)
- picture of a three-leaf clover (clover.jpg)
- counters
- paper plates
- crackers
- colored pencils or highlighters

1 Hold up a picture of a tricycle and a three-leaf clover. Ask students what these two things have in common with each other. Let students talk with a partner and share out as a class that both items have three of something.

2 Tell students that you are thinking of something that comes in twos. Give students clues such as "sometimes we put glasses on these" and "they help us to see" *(eyes)*. Draw a picture of a person. Beside the picture, write *two eyes*. Then draw another picture below that of two people. Beside this picture, write *four eyes*. Keep this going and see if students can predict what number is going to come next. Ask questions such as: If I draw three people, how many eyes will there be all together? How is the total number of eyes changing as we add people to the picture?

3 Ask students to think of something that comes in twos. Ask them to think-pair-share with their partner. Listen to your students' thinking while they are sharing. Provide English language learners with more specific examples. Show them what you are thinking of in the classroom. Ask a few students to share their examples.

4 Have four students come to the front. Ask the class the following questions: How many total legs are there? What number can we count by other than one? What if there were five people? What if there were six people?

5 Draw or show your students a plate with three crackers on it. Ask students how many crackers there would be if there were two plates with three crackers each. Distribute at least six counters and one paper plate to each student. Ask students to use the counters to show you how many crackers would be on two plates if there were three crackers on each plate. Observe closely to determine students' differentiation needs. Clarify and ask questions to help students understand the problem.

6 Pair students with homogeneous partners and distribute the *Crackers for All* activity sheets (pages 84–86) and *Hundred Chart* (page 87) to each pair based on their readiness levels.

Extending Patterns

7 Encourage students to draw and verbally explain their thinking. Have counters available for student use. Read the directions to the class and answer any questions students have. Each pair will work together to solve the math problem. Be prepared to read the math problem aloud to pairs that need assistance.

★ **English Language Support**—Meet with your English language learners in a small group. Go over the directions again with them and check to make sure they understand the problem and the task.

8 If students finish early, they may complete the Anchor Activity.

Assessment

Meet with all of the groups as they work on their activity sheets, taking anecdotal notes about their learning. When the activity is complete, go over the patterns (twos, threes, and fours) by highlighting them on the hundred chart. Have students clap on unhighlighted numbers and snap on highlighted numbers. Ask them what they notice about the patterns and what number is repeating. Ask students if they can extend the twos, threes, and fours pattern further. Take notes on your observations of each student.

Activity Levels
▲
Above Grade Level
■
On Grade Level
●
Below Grade Level

Anchor Activity

Have students look for additional patterns on a hundred chart. Each pattern should be shaded with a different color. Challenge students to look for as many patterns as they can find on the hundred chart.

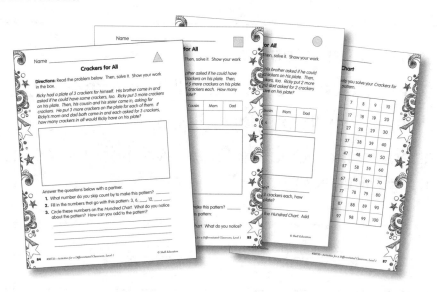

Name _____

Crackers for All

Directions: Read the problem below. Then, solve it. Show your work in the box.

Ricky had a plate of 3 crackers for himself. His brother came in and asked if he could have some crackers, too. Ricky put 3 more crackers on his plate. Then, his cousin and his sister came in, asking for crackers. He put 3 more crackers on the plate for each of them. If Ricky's mom and dad both came in and each asked for 3 crackers, how many crackers in all would Ricky have on his plate?

Answer the questions below with a partner.

1. What number do you skip count by to make this pattern? _____

2. Fill in the numbers that go with this pattern: 3, 6, ___, 12, ___, ___.

3. Circle these numbers on the *Hundred Chart*. What do you notice about the pattern? How can you add to the pattern?

_____
_____
_____
_____

Name _____

Crackers for All

Directions: Read the problem below. Then, solve it. Show your work in the box.

Ricky had a plate of 5 crackers. His brother asked if he could have some crackers, too. Ricky put 5 more crackers on his plate. Then, his cousin asked for crackers. Ricky put 5 more crackers on his plate. Then, Ricky's mom and dad asked for 5 crackers each. How many crackers in all does Ricky have on his plate?

People	Ricky	Brother	Cousin	Mom	Dad
Number of Total Crackers	5				

Answer the questions below with a partner.

1. What number do you skip count by to make this pattern? _____

2. Fill in the numbers that go along with this pattern:
   5, 10, _____, 20, _____.

3. Circle these numbers on the *Hundred Chart*. What do you notice? Add on to the pattern.

Name _____

Crackers for All

Directions: Read the problem below. Then, solve it. Show your work in the box.

Ricky had a plate with 2 crackers on it. His brother asked if he could have some crackers. Ricky put 2 more crackers on his plate. Then, his cousin asked for some of Ricky's crackers, too. Ricky put 2 more crackers on his plate. Then, his mom and dad asked for 2 crackers each. How many crackers does Ricky have on his plate?

Follow this pattern.

People	Ricky	Brother	Cousin	Mom	Dad
Number of Total Crackers	2	4	6		

Show your work here:

Answer the questions below with a partner.

1. What number is repeating in this problem? _____

2. If 2 more people came in and asked for 2 crackers each, how many total crackers would be on Ricky's plate?

   _____

3. Circle the numbers in the chart above on the *Hundred Chart*. Add on to the pattern.

Name _____

Hundred Chart

Directions: Use this hundred chart to help you solve your *Crackers for All* problem. Circle the number in your pattern.

1	2	3	4	5	6	7	8	9	10
11	12	13	14	15	16	17	18	19	20
21	22	23	24	25	26	27	28	29	30
31	32	33	34	35	36	37	38	39	40
41	42	43	44	45	46	47	48	49	50
51	52	53	54	55	56	57	58	59	60
61	62	63	64	65	66	67	68	69	70
71	72	73	74	75	76	77	78	79	80
81	82	83	84	85	86	87	88	89	90
91	92	93	94	95	96	97	98	99	100

Time

Differentiation Strategy

 Menu of Options

Standards

- Students will understand the concept of time and how it is measured.

- TESOL: Students will use English to obtain, process, construct, and provide subject matter information in spoken and written form.

Materials

- lesson resources (pages 90–93)
- analog and digital clocks
- chart paper and markers
- paper plates
- brads
- scissors
- glue
- construction paper
- index cards

1 Before this lesson, give students the *Telling Time Pre-Test* activity sheet (page 90) to evaluate students' readiness levels. Then, make adjustments to your lesson or add scaffolding for students who need it.

2 Begin by asking students what they think they can do in one minute. Share a few responses as a whole class. Pick one of the students' ideas and have the class try it. One idea might be to have them do 25 jumping jacks. After the class attempts to finish this task in one minute, let students revise their thinking and share a few more ideas of things that can happen in a minute.

3 Put students into small groups and distribute analog clocks. Have students brainstorm what they notice about these clocks (as well as the analog clock in the classroom), listing everything they can think of. If students struggle with this, ask questions to get them thinking in the right direction. In what direction are the hands moving? What do you see? Also ask students this question: How do we use clocks to tell time? Discuss everything that was noticed, and make a class chart about telling time. This chart can be used throughout the unit.

4 Clarify basics about the parts of the clock. Explain the functions of the hour and minute hands and how to read a clock to the hour and half-hour. Tell students that when the minute hand moves from one tick mark to another, one minute has passed. Model various examples to the hour and half-hour.

5 Have students make their own clocks to practice telling time. Distribute the *Telling Time Clock Template* activity sheet (page 91), a paper plate, and a brad to each student. Have students cut out the clock face and hands. Students should glue the clock face to the paper plate and use a brad to attach the hands to the paper plate at its center. Model this for students and let students write in the hours following your model. Students will gain a better understanding of the clock parts if they create their own clock.

★ **English Language Support**—Provide an example clock to your English language learners with the names of each part listed on the clock. Check for understanding by having students model different times for you in a small group while others are working on constructing their clocks.

6 Call out different times (in hour or half-hour increments) to the whole class and have students use their own clocks to show you that time. Have students compare their answer with a neighbor. Walk around the room to check for understanding. Use a digital clock to show students a time (half-hour and hour) and ask students to show the time on the analog clock. Ask students what time it is if the large hand is on the six and the small hand is between the eight and the nine. Give more examples like this so that students understand that the hour hand sits between two numbers at the half-hour mark.

7 Distribute copies of the *Telling Time Menu of Options* activity sheet (page 92) to students. Read the options aloud to students, explaining the activities and answering students' questions. Have students choose at least two activities to complete.

8 If students finish early, they may complete the Anchor Activity.

Assessment

To assess students' work, complete a *Telling Time Assessment* (page 93) for each student.

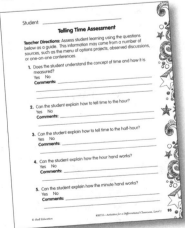

Anchor Activity

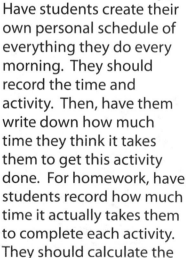

Have students create their own personal schedule of everything they do every morning. They should record the time and activity. Then, have them write down how much time they think it takes them to get this activity done. For homework, have students record how much time it actually takes them to complete each activity. They should calculate the totals and compare these to their estimates.

Telling Time Pre-Test

Directions: Answer the questions about time.

1. What time is it?_____

2. What time is it?_____

3. Draw 1:00

4. Draw 5:00

5. What time is it?_____

6. What time is it?_____

7. Draw 7:30

8. Draw 2:30

Name _____

Telling Time Clock Template

Directions: Cut out the clock and hands below. Follow the teacher's example and write the numbers on the clock. Glue the clock face to a paper plate. Put the hour and minute hand on the clock with a brad.

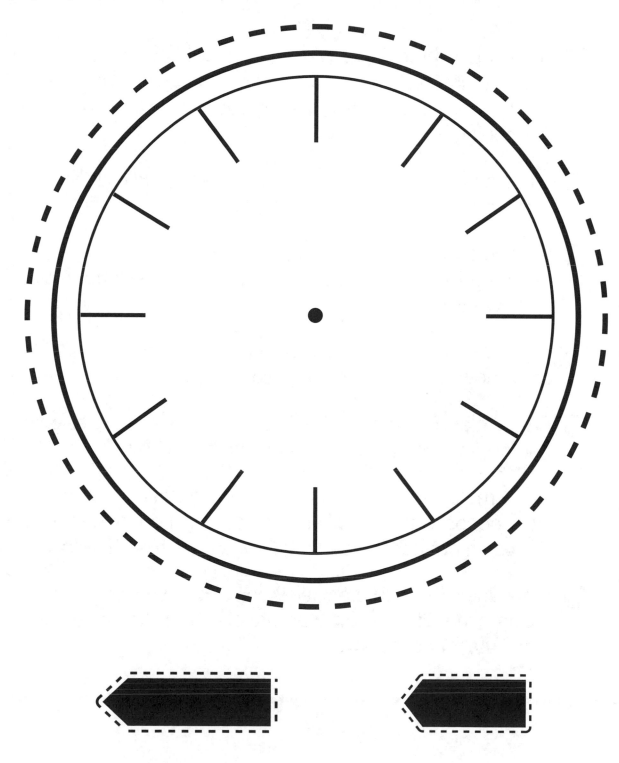

Name _____

Telling Time Menu of Options

Directions: Choose two activities from the list below. Put a checkmark (✔) next to the two you choose.

☐ Think about three things you do every day. Put them in order from the greatest amount of time used to the least amount of time used. How many minutes does it take to do all of these things?

☐ Make a poster about time. Explain how to read a clock, including the minute and hour hands.

☐ Pretend a clock could talk. How would it explain how to tell time? Draw a picture of a clock. Draw speech bubbles. Write what it would say.

☐ Make a mini book using 5 index cards. Your book should show how to tell time on an analog clock.

☐ Create a schedule of a school day with six events. Use both analog and digital clocks to show the correct time.

☐ Make matching picture cards of 10 analog clocks. Each clock needs to show a different time to the hour or half-hour. Choose a partner to play *Time Concentration* or *Go Fish*.

☐ Write down three different television shows you watch and the time they start. Draw a picture of a clock that shows the start time for each show.

Student: _____

Telling Time Assessment

Teacher Directions: Assess student learning using the questions below as a guide. This information may come from a number of sources, such as the menu of options projects, observed discussions, or one-on-one conferences.

1. Does the student understand the concept of time and how it is measured?
   Yes   No
   Comments: _____
   _____
   _____

2. Can the student explain how to tell time to the hour?
   Yes   No
   Comments: _____
   _____

3. Can the student explain how to tell time to the half-hour?
   Yes   No
   Comments: _____
   _____

4. Can the student explain how the hour hand works?
   Yes   No
   Comments: _____
   _____

5. Can the student explain how the minute hand works?
   Yes   No
   Comments: _____
   _____

Weather

Differentiation Strategy

 **Three-Story Intellect**

Standards

- Students will understand that short-term weather conditions can change daily, and weather patterns change over the seasons.

- TESOL: Students will use English to obtain, process, construct, and provide subject matter information in spoken and written form.

Materials

- lesson resources (pages 96–99)

- chart paper and markers

- children's books about weather *(See page 167.)*

- hot plate or microwave

- water

❶ Tell students that weather is the condition of the outside air at a specific time and place. Keep a chart documenting the daily temperature and weather conditions over several weeks. Or, clip the weather forecasts from a newspaper to show students. Ask students what they notice about the changes each day.

❷ Read a children's book that discusses weather and the changes in seasons. Discuss what students notice about seasons and weather from this book. Discuss how snowflakes are made from moisture in the air. Tell students that snowflakes are formed in the clouds and are a type of water (ice). Water evaporates from Earth and gathers up (accumulates) in the clouds, and when it freezes, it becomes snow.

❸ Heat a cup of water in the microwave or on a hot plate to demonstrate water evaporating into the air because it is heated. Point out the steam. Discuss how this happens all the time as part of the water cycle, and tell students that when this happens and it is cold enough (32 degrees Fahrenheit or 0 degrees Celsius or below), snow can be created in the clouds from this moisture.

❹ Ask students what they think will happen if it is warmer than 32 degrees Fahrenheit (or 0 degrees Celsius) and there is a lot of moisture in the air. Give them a chance to talk with partners about their thoughts. Walk around and listen to students' discussions. Allow partners to share their ideas with the class.

5 Place students with homogeneous partners. Distribute copies of the *Weather Changes Daily* activity sheets (pages 96–98) to students based on their readiness levels.

These activities use the Three-Story Intellect Model to differentiate types of questions. The below-grade-level students will be answering Level I questions. On-grade-level students will be answering Level I, II, and III questions. Above-grade-level students will be answering Level II and III questions.

★ **English Language Support**—Explain the directions for their activities to English language learners and answer any questions that students have. Talk about the class weather chart and have students explain what they see and notice on the chart. Read through the questions as a small group and clarify what they should do for their activities.

6 If students finish early, they may complete the Anchor Activity.

Assessment

Observe students in their partner discussions and ask them clarifying questions. Document students' understanding using the *Weather Assessment Checklist* (page 99).

Activity Levels
▲
Above Grade Level
■
On Grade Level
●
Below Grade Level

Anchor Activity

Have students create their own weather book about different kinds of weather. Provide numerous picture books about weather and paper for creating booklets for students. They should draw pictures and show what the temperature might be during each type of weather. Give students the opportunity to share their books with other students.

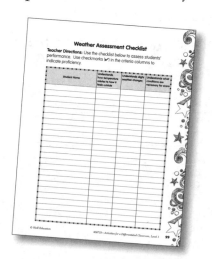

Name _____

Weather Changes Daily

Directions: Use the class weather chart to answer the questions below.

1. What patterns do you notice in the class weather chart?

   _____

   _____

2. How has the weather changed over the last week?

   _____

   _____

3. What do you think the weather will be like tomorrow?

   _____

   _____

4. What do you think the weather will be like over the next few days?

   _____

   _____

   Why? _____

   _____

5. What would need to happen to the weather for it to snow tomorrow?

   _____

   _____

6. What would need to happen to the weather so that we could swim tomorrow?

   _____

   _____

Name _____

Weather Changes Daily

Directions: Use the class weather chart to answer the
questions below.

1. What was the highest temperature on the class weather chart?

   _____

2. What was the lowest temperature on the class weather chart?

   _____

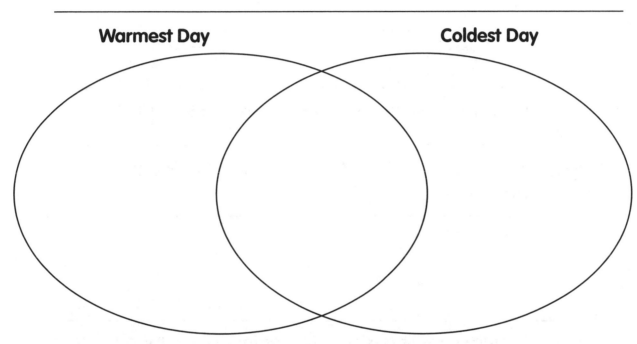

Warmest Day   **Coldest Day**

3. Fill in the Venn diagram to show how the warmest day and the
   coldest day were alike and how they were different.

4. Was it cold enough to snow? If it was not cold enough to snow,
   why not? _____

5. What do you think the weather will be like tomorrow?

   _____

   _____

6. If the temperature dropped below 32°F, what do you think
   might happen?

   _____

   _____

Name _____

Weather Changes Daily

Directions: Use the class weather chart to answer the questions.

1. What was the highest temperature on the class weather chart? _____

    Draw a picture to show what the weather was like on the warmest day.

2. What was the lowest temperature on the class weather chart? _____

    Draw a picture to show what the weather was like on the coldest day.

3. Draw a picture showing what the weather is like today.

4. Draw a picture next to each thermometer. Show what the weather would be like at that temperature.

    88°

    20°

Weather Assessment Checklist

Teacher Directions: Use the checklist below to assess students' performance. Use checkmarks (✔) in the criteria columns to indicate proficiency.

Student Name	Understands how temperature relates to how it feels outside	Understands slight weather changes	Understands what conditions are necessary for snow

Where Does the Moon Go?

Differentiation Strategy

Multiple Intelligences

Standards

• Students will know basic patterns of the sun and moon.

• TESOL: Students will use English to obtain, process, construct, and provide subject matter information in spoken and written form.

Materials

• lesson resources (pages 102–105)

• pictures of moon phases (moonphases.jpg)

• flashlight

• large ball

• science journals (optional)

1 Engage students by asking, "Where does the moon go when we can't see it?" Let students share their ideas with a partner. Explain that the moon is always there, but whether we can see it depends on its location in relation to Earth and the sun.

2 Display pictures of the moon phases. Tell students that the moon goes through different phases. Ask students what they notice about the change from new moon to first-quarter moon. Give them time to talk with a partner. Tell students that these pictures were taken over the course of one month. Explain to students that the moon is Earth's closest neighbor in space, that it orbits Earth, and that together the moon and Earth both orbit the stationary sun.

3 Explain that the moon still exists and keeps orbiting Earth even if it cannot be seen. Remind students that the moon does not make its own light or heat like the sun. We can only see the moon because the sun's light shines on it. If the moon is between the sun and Earth, we will not be able to see it completely and not at all at times. This is because the sun is shining on the *other* side of the moon, the side that is not visible to us.

4 Using a flashlight to represent the sun, a ball to represent the moon, and yourself as Earth, put the ball between your face and the light to show how you cannot see the moon because the sun is shining on the *other* side of the moon, away from you. Point out the picture of a new moon, telling students that even though we cannot see it, it is still there.

5 Explain that, if Earth is between the sun and the moon, we can see the entire moon (a full moon), because the sun is shining on the side of the moon that is facing us. Move so you are between the light (sun) and the ball (moon), showing students that the sun can shine on the moon, making it visible to us through reflection. If it is a clear day, you can sometimes see the moon during the day. Also model half moon and crescent moon.

6 Give students time to ask questions. Then, ask clarifying questions, such as: Why does the moon look different at different times of the month? What phase is it when the moon seems to disappear? What phase is it when we can see the whole moon? Provide time for students to think-pair-share.

Where Does the Moon Go?

7 Keep the moon phases images displayed for students. Then, have students draw each of these and label the phases in their science journals.

★ **English Language Support**—Talk to English language learners to check for understanding and have them verbalize their learning so that you can determine if they need more time with this concept before moving on to a project.

8 Tell students that they are going to show what they have learned about the moon by selecting a project to complete.

9 Explain each of the three activity sheets. The *Moon Time Line* activity sheet (page 102) addresses the logical/mathematical intelligence. The *Moon Talk* activity sheet (page 103) addresses the verbal/linguistic intelligence. The *Moon Acts* activity sheet (page 104) addresses the bodily/kinesthetic intelligence. Have students choose a partner and together select one activity sheet to complete.

10 If students finish early, they may complete the Anchor Activity.

Assessment

To assess students' understanding, complete the *Moon Activities Rubric* (page 105).

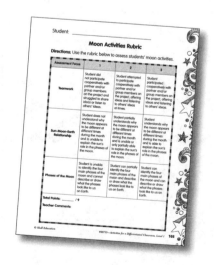

Anchor Activity ⚓

Have students respond in writing to the following questions:

• Are the moon phases the same if you are living in a country on the other side of the world instead of your country? Why or why not?

• Do you believe there is life on the moon? If so, what kind of life? If not, why not?

Name _____

Moon Time Line

Directions: Answer the questions about the moon.

1. Why can you see the whole moon in this picture?

   _____

   _____

2. Why can you only see part of the moon in these pictures?

   _____

   _____

3. Why is the moon invisible in this picture?

   _____

   _____

4. Fill in the time line below showing how the moon changes. Draw pictures on your time line.

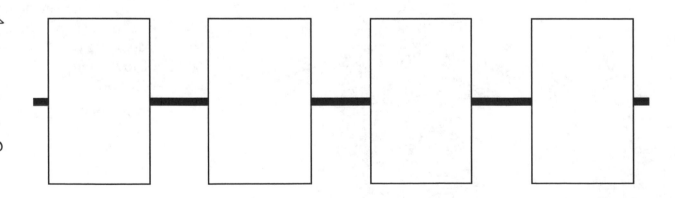

Name _____

Moon Talk

Directions: The moon wants to tell about its four phases. In each of the speech bubbles, draw a different phase and write what the moon would say about it.

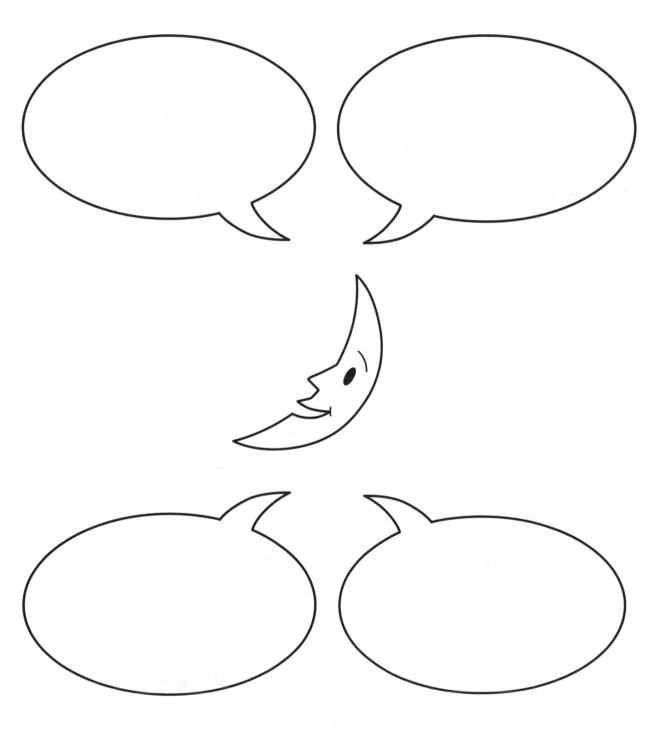

Name _____

Moon Acts

Directions: Make up a skit to act out the phases of the moon. Tell about the phases of the moon in your skit. Answer the questions below before planning your skit.

1. What will you say about the new moon phase?

   _____

   _____

   _____

2. What will you say about the first-quarter moon phase?

   _____

   _____

   _____

3. What will you say about the third-quarter moon phase?

   _____

   _____

   _____

4. What will you say about the full moon phase?

   _____

   _____

   _____

5. How will you act? Use the back of this sheet to plan your skit. Practice your skit.

Student: _____

Moon Activities Rubric

Directions: Use the rubric below to assess students' moon activities.

Assessment Focus	1	2	3
Teamwork	Student did not participate cooperatively with partner and/or group members on the project and struggled to share ideas or listen to others' ideas.	Student attempted to participate cooperatively with partner and/or group members on the project, offering ideas and listening to others' ideas at times.	Student participated cooperatively with partner and/or group members on the project, offering ideas and listening to others' ideas.
Sun-Moon-Earth Relationship	Student does not understand why the moon appears to be different at different times during the month and is unable to explain the sun's role in the phases of the moon.	Student partially understands why the moon appears to be different at different times during the month and is unable or only partially able to explain the sun's role in the phases of the moon.	Student understands why the moon appears to be different at different times during the month and is able to explain the sun's role in the phases of the moon.
Phases of the Moon	Student is unable to identify the four main phases of the moon and cannot describe or draw what the phases look like to us on Earth.	Student can partially identify the four main phases of the moon and describe or draw what the phases look like to us on Earth.	Student can identify the four main phases of the moon and can describe or draw what the phases look like to us on Earth.

Total Points: _____ / 9

Teacher Comments:

Plants

Differentiation Strategy

 Open-Ended Tasks

Standards

• Students will know that plants need certain resources for energy and growth such as food, water, light, and air.

• TESOL: Students will use English to obtain, process, construct, and provide subject matter information in spoken and written form.

Materials

• lesson resources (pages 108–111)

• children's books about plants *(See page 167.)*

• a dead plant or a picture of one (plant.jpg)

• bean seeds

• plastic storage bags

• paper towels

• tape

❶ Ask students what they think are the most important things a plant needs to live. Have students work in pairs to make a list. Have partners share their lists with the class.

❷ Share a children's book about plants and the resources they need to survive. Make a list of resources as a class and discuss what would happen if a plant did not have these resources.

❸ Have students use a science journal or paper to record their thinking. Bring out a dead plant (or a picture of one). Ask students what they think happened to this plant. Write their responses on the board. Make a list on the board about what is known about this plant. Answer all questions that students have, making sure to answer "No" when they ask if the plant had been watered daily. If students do not ask about this or other resources, point out the class chart and remind them to ask about these things. Tell students that the plant has not been watered for the last six days.

❹ Pose this question: "Why did this plant die?" Remind students to look back at the board about what is known and use this to help decide what happened to this plant.

❺ Write the word *hypothesis* on the board. Tell students they are going to create a hypothesis and test it. Tell them that a hypothesis is a guess about something that will happen. Also explain that they should have a reason for their guess. Model how to write a hypothesis: *If this plant has _____, it will continue to grow.*

❻ Distribute copies of the *What a Plant Really Needs Hypothesis* activity sheet (page 108) to students. Have students look at the facts on the board and think about what happened to this plant. Clarify that this plant did not get water and that we need to write a hypothesis based on this. Guide students in writing the following hypothesis: If a plant does not get water, it will die.

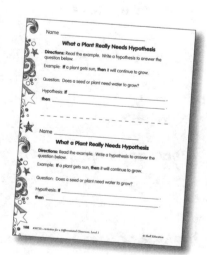

7 Students will grow one plant, such as a lima bean, in a plastic storage bag. Distribute a seed, a storage bag, and a wet paper towel to each student. Have students wrap the seed in the wet paper towel and place it in the bag. Help them to tape it to a window where it can receive sunlight. Label the plants with students' names. Prepare one extra seed in the same manner but do not water it. This plant will be called the class plant.

8 Distribute copies of the *Plant Observation* activity sheet (page 109) to students on the first day so that students can begin to record data and guide their work. Make sure students water and check their plants daily. They need to be sure to wet the paper towels each day so that the seed has enough water to grow.

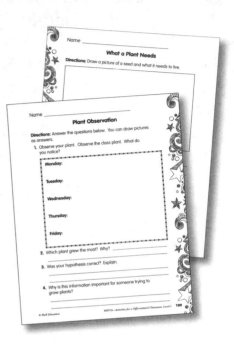

9 Distribute copies of the *What a Plant Needs* activity sheet (page 110) to students. Give students time to work on this and ask questions. After five days, students should be able to see the roots and the stem growing on the plant. Be sure to explain that eventually these seeds will need soil.

★ **English Language Support**—Read over the questions and use pictures and gestures with your English language learners to ensure they understand these concepts.

10 If students finish early, they may complete the Anchor Activity.

Assessment

After finishing their projects, have students complete the *Plants Self-Assessment* (page 111).

Anchor Activity

Have students read various picture books on plants, taking notes while they read. Have them complete a *KWL* chart to help them guide their research so that they can share what they have learned once they are finished.

Name _____

What a Plant Really Needs Hypothesis

Directions: Read the example. Write a hypothesis to answer the question below.

Example: **If** a plant gets sun, **then** it will continue to grow.

Question: Does a seed or plant need water to grow?

Hypothesis: **If** _____ ,

then _____ .

- -

Name _____

What a Plant Really Needs Hypothesis

Directions: Read the example. Write a hypothesis to answer the question below.

Example: **If** a plant gets sun, **then** it will continue to grow.

Question: Does a seed or plant need water to grow?

Hypothesis: **If** _____ ,

then _____ .

Name _____

Plant Observation

Directions: Answer the questions below. You can draw pictures
as answers.

1. Observe your plant. Observe the class plant. What do
    you notice?

Monday:

Tuesday:

Wednesday:

Thursday:

Friday:

2. Which plant grew the most? Why? _____
    _____

3. Was your hypothesis correct? Explain.
    _____
    _____

4. Why is this information important for someone trying to
    grow plants?
    _____
    _____

Name _____

What a Plant Needs

Directions: Draw a picture of a seed and what it needs to live.

Directions: Pretend you are the seed. Tell about what you need to live. _____

_____

_____

_____

_____

_____

_____

_____

Name _____

Plants Self-Assessment

Part 1 Directions: Circle or color the face that describes your work.

1. I wrote an "if-then" hypothesis.	☺	😐	☹
2. My hypothesis included how a plant needs water.	☺	😐	☹
3. I checked my plant and gave it water every day.	☺	😐	☹
4. I observed my plant and the class plant every day.	☺	😐	☹
5. I recorded my observations about the plants every day.	☺	😐	☹

Part 2 Directions: Write what you liked and did not like about the plant project on the lines below.

_____

_____

_____

_____

_____

How Do Birds Eat?

Differentiation Strategy

 Leveled Learning Centers

Standards

• Students will know that plants and animals have features that help them live in different environments.

• TESOL: Students will use English to obtain, process, construct, and provide subject matter information in spoken and written form.

Materials

• lesson resources (pages 114–117)

• tweezers

• scissors

• drinking straws

• pliers

• cooked spaghetti

• cups

• water

• beef jerky

• sunflower seeds

Preparation Note: Set up four centers in the classroom. Place tweezers, drinking straws, scissors, pliers, lined paper, and pencils at all of the centers. Make copies of the *Spaghetti Center* and *Beef Jerky Center* activity sheet (page 115) and the *Liquid Center* and *Seeds Center* activity sheet (page 116). Cut the copies apart and place them at the appropriate centers. Place the cooked spaghetti, beef jerky, cups of water, and sunflower seeds at the appropriate centers.

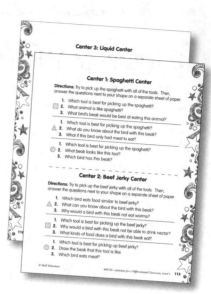

1 Begin by asking students to show how they eat their food. Students should act this out without talking. Depending on what they are eating, some might eat with their hands and others might eat with utensils.

2 Ask students to think about their favorite foods. Write these foods on the board. Ask these questions: What if we did not have any teeth? Could we still eat these foods? What foods would we have to eat if we did not have teeth? List students' answers on the board.

3 Ask these questions: Why do animals eat different kinds of foods? Have a few students share their thinking. Do animals' teeth and mouths have anything to do with what they eat? Tell students that they are going to do some experiments to find out.

4 Distribute copies of the *Different Kinds of Birds* activity sheet (page 114) to students or display the page so the class can see it. Ask students if they have ever watched birds eat. If so, let them act out how birds eat. Ask: What is the difference between how we eat and how birds eat? How are these birds different from one another?

How Do Birds Eat?

5 Assign students a shape based on their readiness levels.

★ **English Language Support**—Pair these learners with language-proficient students who are at their same academic readiness level. These student pairs will visit the different learning centers and work together.

6 Tell students that they will be visiting four different centers. Explain that students will try to pick up the food at each center, using all the different tools. They will decide which tool works best for each food type. Then, they will complete the questions that match the shape you assigned them.

7 Divide the class into four groups and assign each group to a center. Give students time to complete the work at each center and then have the groups rotate to new centers. Repeat this until all students have visited the four centers.

8 Bring students back together. Display the *Different Kinds of Birds* activity sheet (page 114) again. Have a class discussion about how the tools represent the birds' beaks in the pictures the class studied: scissors—sharp like an eagle's beak; tweezers—long and thin, like a woodpecker's beak; pliers—able to grab and crush like a finch's beak; straws—very long and thin, like a hummingbird's beak. Also, discuss what the food items at the centers represent in real life: water—nectar; beef jerky—meat; spaghetti—worms and insects; seeds—nuts and seeds.

9 If students finish early, they may complete the Anchor Activity.

Assessment

As students work in each of the centers, walk around and observe their work and ask questions to see if they understand the concepts at each center. You may also wish to use the *Birds' Beaks Assessment* (page 117) to record how well students understand the concepts.

Activity Levels
▲
Above Grade Level
■
On Grade Level
●
Below Grade Level

Anchor Activity ⚓

Have students make up a new bird with a certain kind of beak. Then, have them decide what kinds of food this new bird would or could eat. They should give their bird a name, list some facts about it, and then create a trading card for their bird with all this information on it.

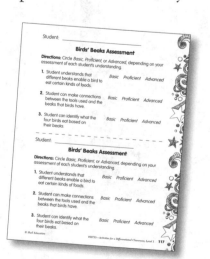

Name _____

Different Kinds of Birds

Directions: Look at these birds. How are their beaks different? Think about why their beaks are different.

Golden Eagle	Hummingbird

Woodpecker	Finch

Center 1: Spaghetti Center

Directions: Try to pick up the spaghetti with all of the tools. Then, answer the questions next to your shape on a separate sheet of paper.

1. Which tool is best for picking up the spaghetti?
2. What animal is like spaghetti?
3. What bird's beak would be best at eating this animal?

---

1. Which tool is best for picking up the spaghetti?
2. What do you know about the bird with this beak?
3. What if this bird only had meat to eat?

---

1. Which tool is best for picking up the spaghetti?
2. What beak looks like this tool?
3. Which bird has this beak?

- -

Center 2: Beef Jerky Center

Directions: Try to pick up the beef jerky with all of the tools. Then, answer the questions next to your shape on a separate sheet of paper.

1. Which bird eats food similar to beef jerky?
2. What do you know about the bird with this type of beak?
3. Why would a bird with this beak not eat worms?

---

1. Which tool is best for picking up the beef jerky?
2. Why would a bird with this beak not be able to drink nectar?
3. What kinds of food does a bird with this beak eat?

---

1. Which tool is best for picking up beef jerky?
2. Draw the beak that this tool is like.
3. Which bird eats meat?

Center 3: Liquid Center

Directions: Try to pick up the water with all of the tools. Then, answer the questions next to your shape on a separate sheet of paper.

1. Which tool is best for picking up the water?
2. What kind of beak looks like this tool?
3. What do you know about the bird with this beak?

1. Which tool is best for picking up the water?
2. Which bird has a beak like this tool?
3. What if this bird only had beef jerky to eat? What would happen?

1. Which tool is best for picking up the water?
2. What kind of beak looks like this tool?
3. Which bird drinks nectar?

Center 4: Seeds Center

Directions: Try to pick up the seeds with all of the tools. Then, answer the questions next to your shape on a separate sheet of paper.

1. Which tool is best for picking up the seeds?
2. In what ways does this tool look like a bird's beak?
3. What would happen if a bird with this beak had only nectar to drink?

1. Which tool is best for picking up the seeds?
2. Why does this tool work best?
3. Which bird's beak looks like this tool?

1. Which tool is best for picking up the seeds?
2. What does this tell us about the type of bird that eats seeds?
3. What would happen if this bird had only worms to eat?

Student: _____

Birds' Beaks Assessment

Directions: Circle *Basic, Proficient,* or *Advanced,* depending on your assessment of each student's understanding.

1. Student understands that different beaks enable a bird to eat certain kinds of foods.   *Basic   Proficient   Advanced*

2. Student can make connections between the tools used and the beaks that birds have.   *Basic   Proficient   Advanced*

3. Student can identify what the four birds eat based on their beaks.   *Basic   Proficient   Advanced*

— —

Student: _____

Birds' Beaks Assessment

Directions: Circle *Basic, Proficient,* or *Advanced,* depending on your assessment of each student's understanding.

1. Student understands that different beaks enable a bird to eat certain kinds of foods.   *Basic   Proficient   Advanced*

2. Student can make connections between the tools used and the beaks that birds have.   *Basic   Proficient   Advanced*

3. Student can identify what the four birds eat based on their beaks.   *Basic   Proficient   Advanced*

Scientists Observe and Experiment!

Differentiation Strategy

 Menu of Options

Standards

- Students will know that learning can come from careful observations and simple experiments.

- TESOL: Students will use English to obtain, process, construct, and provide subject matter information in spoken and written form.

Materials

- lesson resources (pages 120–123)

- chart paper and markers

- science journals

- a variety of rocks

- plastic containers

- items to test for sink or float effects

- ice

- index cards

- audio recorder

1 Ask students what a scientist is. Give students time to talk with a partner and have them share their ideas with the class. Consider having students draw a picture of a scientist. This will provide excellent information about students' understanding and beliefs about what a scientist is or is not. Tell students that scientists learn new things by carefully observing and conducting simple experiments. Explain that they are going to be scientists and that they will need to think like scientists.

2 Tell students that scientists are people who are curious, ask questions, and wonder about how things work. Ask students to think about things that they are curious about. Provide a few suggestions to get them started and write these on a class chart. An example might be: *I am curious and want to know what the fastest way to melt an ice cube is.* Give students time to record some ideas in their science journals and to share their ideas with a partner. While students are sharing, listen to and observe their thinking processes. They can also add more to this list after they share.

3 Tell students this is a list they will come back to throughout the year. Make sure the class list includes some wonderings that could easily be turned into simple experiments in the classroom. Ask a few students to share their thoughts and add these to your class chart.

4 Distribute copies of the *Scientists Experiment Menu of Options* activity sheet (page 120) and the *Menu of Options Experiment Planning Chart* activity sheet (page 121) to students. Explain the activities to students. Tell students to think about which activities they would like to do. Instruct students to record their experiment choice(s) and complete the rest of the *Menu of Options Experiment Planning Chart*. The planning chart can be used for any experiment. Explain to students how you want them to complete the chart. Point out that they will need to make a prediction before they start to do the experiment. Make sure you have gathered materials in advance for students to use during experiments.

Scientists Observe and Experiment!

5 Group students together based on their choice of experiment. Help students with the planning process. If students change what they are planning to do, they should let you know. Distribute copies of the *Menu of Options Experiment Sheet* activity sheet (page 122) for students to fill out as they conduct their experiment.

6 Distribute copies of the *Menu of Options Observation Sheet* activity sheet (page 123) and have students choose to do either the *Rock Sorting Activity* or the *Living and Nonliving Scavenger Hunt*. For the students who choose to do the *Living and Nonliving Scavenger Hunt*, plan to take them out as a group during recess or arrange for a parent volunteer to supervise the scavenger hunt.

★ **English Language Support**—If possible, make an audio recording of the information on the menu of options activity sheet so that these students can listen to it several times. Make modifications if necessary to allow these students to complete their work orally or by drawing pictures.

7 If students finish early, they may complete the Anchor Activity.

Assessment

To assess students' understanding, have them answer these questions in their science journals by writing and drawing their thoughts: What have you learned about being a scientist? What have you learned about simple experiments?

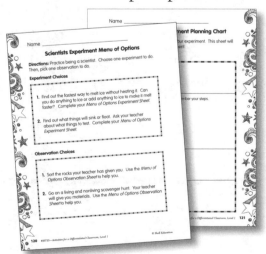

Anchor Activity

Have students make a sign advertising the job of a scientist. The sign should explain the job in an exciting way.

Name _____

Scientists Experiment Menu of Options

Directions: Practice being a scientist. Choose one experiment to do. Then, pick one observation to do.

Experiment Choices

1. Find out the fastest way to melt ice without heating it. Can you do anything to ice or add anything to ice to make it melt faster? Complete your *Menu of Options Experiment Sheet*.

2. Find out what things will sink or float. Ask your teacher about what things to test. Complete your *Menu of Options Experiment Sheet*.

Observation Choices

1. Sort the rocks your teacher has given you. Use the *Menu of Options Observation Sheet* to help you.

2. Go on a living and nonliving scavenger hunt. Your teacher will give you materials. Use the *Menu of Options Observation Sheet* to help you.

Name _____

Menu of Options Experiment Planning Chart

Directions: Fill in the table below for your experiment. This sheet will help you get ready to do your experiment.

Experiment Choice Number _____

What materials do you need?
What are your steps for this experiment? Number your steps.
What are you trying to find out?
Make a prediction about what will happen.

Name _____

Menu of Options Experiment Sheet

Directions: Fill in this table as you do the experiment. If you have more than five steps, add the rest to another sheet of paper.

Name of Experiment: _____

Prediction	
Step 1 observations and sketch	
Step 2 observations and sketch	
Step 3 observations and sketch	
Step 4 observations and sketch	
Step 5 observations and sketch	

What did you learn by doing this experiment?

_____

_____

Was your prediction correct? Why or why not?

_____

_____

Name _____

Menu of Options Observation Sheet

Directions: Choose your observation. Follow the steps below.

Rock Sorting Observation:

1. Look at the rocks.

2. What do you notice about your rocks? Draw each rock.

```




```

3. Sort your rocks into groups. How did you sort your rocks?

_____

_____

4. Make a pattern with your rocks. Draw your pattern here.

```



```

5. Draw your partner's pattern here.

```



```

Living and Nonliving Scavenger Hunt:

1. Find a partner. Talk about living things. Talk about nonliving things. How are they different? How are they alike?

2. Look for three living things on the playground. Look for three nonliving things on the playground.

3. Draw a picture of these things on index cards. Draw one thing on each card.

4. How do you know if the thing is living or nonliving? Write your answer on the back of the index cards.

Water Changes

Differentiation Strategy

 Tiered Assignments

Standards

- Students know that water can be a liquid or a solid and can be made to change from one form to the other, but the amount of water stays the same.

- TESOL: Students will use English to obtain, process, construct, and provide subject matter information in spoken and written form.

Materials

- lesson resources (pages 126–129)
- ice cubes
- water
- cups
- science journals

Preparation Note: Fill two cups with an equal amount of water. Freeze one of the cups.

1 Tell students that they are going to work as scientists to carefully observe water and learn how it changes. Have students take out science journals or paper for this lesson.

2 Divide the class into heterogeneous groups. Distribute a cup of ice cubes and a cup of water to each group. Ask questions for students to discuss in groups: What is in the cups? What does it look like? What does it feel like? Have students sketch the cups and their contents, adding labels and observations.

3 Ask the following questions about ice: What is ice made of? How is ice made? Pour the ice into a container of a different shape or size. Ask: What does it look like now? Does it look the same or different? What will happen if we leave the ice out for a while? Why? How do you know? How long might it take to change? Have students make predictions and record them in their journals.

★ **English Language Support**—Allow English language learners to draw as much as needed and, if necessary, limit their writing requirement to labels only.

4 Have students describe the water. Ask: What does it look like? What does it feel like? Pour the water into a container of a different shape or size. Ask: What does it look like now? Does it look the same or different? Did you add or lose any water? Has the shape of the water changed? Why do you think that is? Invite students to share their thinking with the whole class.

5 Hold up a cup of water. Ask students what would happen if it were put into a freezer. Bring out a cup of frozen water and tell students that this is the same amount of water. It is now a solid because the temperature was below 32 degrees Fahrenheit (0 degrees Celsius) in the freezer, causing it to change form to a solid. Tell students that when we freeze water, we do not lose any of it. Have students record what they learned about water when it freezes in their science journals.

Water Changes

6 Place students with homogeneous partners. Explain the directions and distribute the *Water Changes Sorting Sheet* activity sheet (page 126). Have students complete the activity.

7 Distribute the *Water Changes* activity sheets (pages 127–129) to students based on their readiness levels.

★ **English Language Support**—Meet with English language learners to introduce or review the vocabulary terms for the pictures on the *Water Changes Sorting Sheet*.

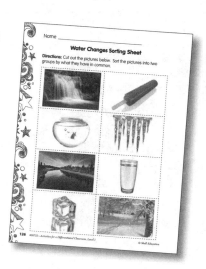

Activity Levels
▲
Above Grade Level
■
On Grade Level
●
Below Grade Level

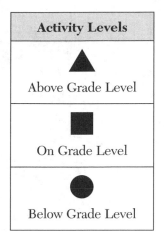

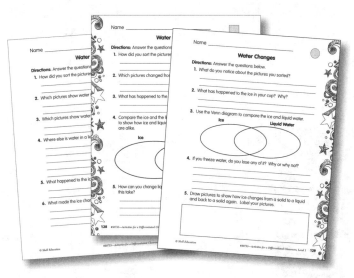

8 If students finish early, they may complete the Anchor Activity.

Assessment

To assess students' understanding, have them answer the following questions in their journal, using words and pictures. Allow English language learners to explain their answers orally. How can we make water change from water to ice? How can we make ice change to water? Give an example of where you would see water going back and forth from one form to another.

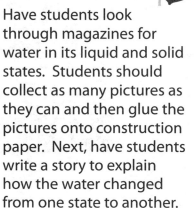

Anchor Activity

Have students look through magazines for water in its liquid and solid states. Students should collect as many pictures as they can and then glue the pictures onto construction paper. Next, have students write a story to explain how the water changed from one state to another.

Name _____

Water Changes Sorting Sheet

Directions: Cut out the pictures below. Sort the pictures into two groups by what they have in common.

Name _____

Water Changes

Directions: Answer the questions below.

1. How did you sort the pictures?

_____

_____

2. Which pictures show water in a solid state?

_____

_____

3. Which pictures show water in a liquid state?

_____

_____

4. Where else is water in a liquid state?

_____

_____

_____

_____

_____

5. What happened to the ice that we left out?

_____

_____

6. What made the ice change?

_____

_____

_____

Name _____

Water Changes

Directions: Answer the questions below.

1. How did you sort the pictures?

_____

_____

2. Which pictures show water as a solid?

_____

_____

3. What has happened to the ice in your cup? Why?

_____

_____

4. Compare the ice and the liquid water. Use the Venn diagram to show how ice and liquid water are different and how they are alike.

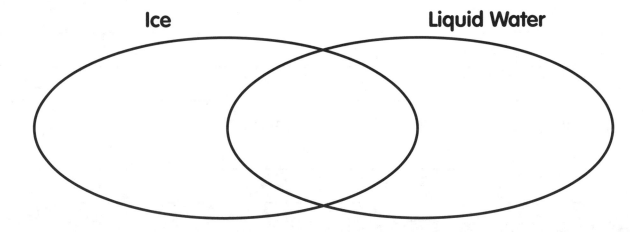

Ice   **Liquid Water**

5. How can you change liquid water back to ice? How long might this take?

_____

_____

_____

Name _____

Water Changes

Directions: Answer the questions below.

1. What do you notice about the pictures you sorted?

_____

_____

2. What has happened to the ice in your cup? Why?

_____

_____

3. Use the Venn diagram to compare the ice and liquid water.

Ice   **Liquid Water**

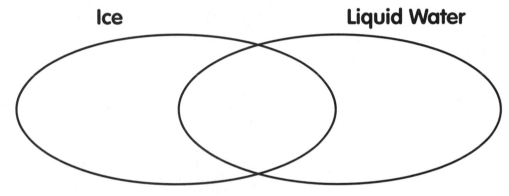

4. If you freeze water, do you lose any of it? Why or why not?

_____

_____

_____

_____

5. Draw pictures to show how ice changes from a solid to a liquid and back to a solid again. Label your pictures.

Family Life and Community

Differentiation Strategy

 Open-Ended Tasks

Standards

• Students will understand family life now and in the past, and family life in various places long ago.

• TESOL: Students will use English to obtain, process, construct, and provide subject matter information in spoken and written form.

Materials

• lesson resources (pages 132–135)

• parent letter requesting family information and family photo

Preparation Note: Before this lesson begins, send a letter home to parents explaining that you will be studying family life. Ask parents to share stories with their child about their family history and the important roles of different family members. Also, ask that they choose a family photo to send to school with their child and write a few sentences telling about the family members in the photo.

❶ Talk about ways that family members are important to each other and how they help each other. Share a family picture to model your thinking to the students. Display one of the student's photographs. Identify whom the picture belongs to and ask students who they think the family members might be. Ask students how a certain person in the photo might be important to the family and what his or her role might be in the family. Then, allow the picture's owner to share information about his or her family.

❷ Distribute copies of the *Family Is Important!* activity sheet (page 132) to students.

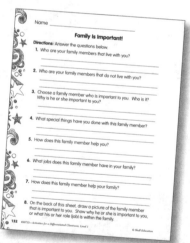

❸ Divide the class into small heterogeneous groups to discuss their families by referring to their activity sheet answers. Tell students to take turns sharing in their groups. Circulate and listen to group discussions.

❹ As a whole group, discuss some of the different responses you heard, and together make a class chart with all of the different types of family members mentioned. Next, ask students to think of one family member that is very important in their life, and why. Model this by sharing a specific example from your own family.

Family Life and Community

5 Distribute copies of the *Questions About Family* activity sheet (page 133) to students. Students can use this sheet to prepare to interview another student in class about a family member and also to prepare to be interviewed themselves.

★ **English Language Support**—Meet with English language learners at this time in a small group. Guide them through this task, making sure they know how to formulate and write the questions.

6 Partner students and give them time to interview each other. Make sure to tell them that they should record what their partner tells them. Explain that they will share their interviews with their classmates.

7 Allow time for students to share with the whole class or in small groups. If they share in small groups, walk around and listen to presentations, and then hold a whole-class discussion to culminate the activity. Following the presentations, have students reflect by recording at least two things that they learned about other students' family lives.

8 If students finish early, they may complete the Anchor Activity.

Assessment

To assess student understanding, listen closely to discussions, interviews, and presentations, and use the *Family Is Important Rubric* (page 134) to assess and share feedback with parents.

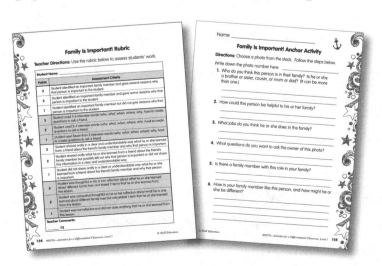

Anchor Activity

Have students complete the *Family Is Important! Anchor Activity* (page 135). Make copies of the photos that were sent to school and return the originals to students. Number the copied photos on the back to keep track of them. Have students choose a photo to write about, write down its number, and then follow the directions on the sheet. Students can compare their predictions to what they find out from their classmates during presentations.

Name _____

Family Is Important!

Directions: Answer the questions below.

1. Who are your family members that live with you?

_____

_____

2. Who are your family members that do not live with you?

_____

_____

3. Choose a family member who is important to you. Who is it?
   Why is he or she important to you?

_____

_____

4. What special things have you done with this family member?

_____

_____

5. How does this family member help you?

_____

_____

6. What jobs does this family member have in your family?

_____

_____

7. How does this family member help your family?

_____

_____

8. On the back of this sheet, draw a picture of the family member
   that is important to you. Show why he or she is important to you,
   or what his or her role (job) is within the family.

Name _____

Questions About Family

Directions: Think of questions to ask a friend about his or her family member.

Good interviewers try to include these types of question words in their questions:

Who?	When?	Why?
What?	Where?	How?

Try to use all of the words above in your questions. Remember, you want to know why that person is important.

Write your questions here. Make sure to number them.

_____

_____

_____

_____

_____

_____

_____

_____

_____

_____

_____

Family Is Important! Rubric

Teacher Directions: Use the rubric below to assess students' work.

Student Name: _____	
Points	**Assessment Criteria**
3	Student identified an important family member and gave several reasons why that person is important to the student.
2	Student identified an important family member and gave some reasons why that person is important to the student.
1	Student identified an important family member but did not give reasons why that person is important to the student.
3	Student used 5–6 interview words (*who, what, when, where, why, how*) to create questions to ask a friend.
2	Student used 2–4 interview words (*who, what, when, where, why, how*) to create questions to ask a friend.
1	Student used fewer than 2 interview words (*who, what, when, where, why, how*) to create questions to ask a friend.
3	Student shared orally in a clear and understandable way what he or she learned from a friend about the friend's family member and why that person is important.
2	Student shared orally what he or she learned from a friend about the friend's family member but possibly left out why that person is important or did not share this information in a clear and understandable way.
1	Student did not share orally in a clear or understandable way what he or she learned from a friend about the friend's family member and why that person is important.
3	Student was thoughtful in his or her reflection about what he or she learned about different family lives and stated 2 items that he or she learned from this lesson.
2	Student was somewhat thoughtful in his or her reflection about what he or she learned about different family lives but only stated 1 item that he or she learned from this lesson.
1	Student was not reflective and did not state anything that he or she learned from this lesson.

Teacher Comments:

_____ /12

Name _____

Family Is Important! Anchor Activity

Directions: Choose a photo from the stack. Follow the steps below.

Write down the photo number here: _____

1. Who do you think this person is in their family? Is he or she a brother or sister, cousin, or mom or dad? (It can be more than one.)

   _____

   _____

2. How could this person be helpful to his or her family?

   _____

   _____

3. What jobs do you think he or she does in the family?

   _____

   _____

4. What questions do you want to ask the owner of this photo?

   _____

   _____

5. Is there a family member with this role in your family?

   _____

   _____

6. How is your family member like this person, and how might he or she be different?

   _____

   _____

   _____

   _____

Changes in Community

Differentiation Strategy

 Three-Story Intellect

Standards

- Students will understand changes in community life over time.

- TESOL: Students will use English to obtain, process, construct, and provide subject matter information in spoken and written form.

Materials

- lesson resources (pages 138–141)

- chart paper and markers

- books about transportation *(See page 167.)*

- art supplies

❶ Ask students how they got to school today. Create a list on a class chart titled *Transportation*. Ask students: What are all the ways that we can travel from one place to another? Have students talk to a partner about this and then discuss more types of transportation to add to your class list.

❷ Ask students to think about these questions: What if we did not have cars or buses or anything that had engines? How would we get around? Give students time to share with a partner and record at least one thought. Share ideas as a class, adding these ideas about transportation to the chart. Talk about why there was a need (before the invention of the car) for these other types of transportation.

★ **English Language Support**—Preteach the vocabulary for the modes of transportation on the *Transportation Then-and-Now Pictures* activity sheet (page 138) so that English language learners can participate in the group activity.

❸ Divide the class into small heterogeneous groups. Distribute a copy of the *Transportation Then-and-Now Pictures* activity sheet (page 138) to each group. Have students cut out the pictures and place them in two groups: "Then" and "Now."

❹ As a class, go over the right answers to make sure students understand which modes of transportation were used in the past and which are used today.

Changes in Community

5 Distribute copies of the *Transportation Then-and-Now* activity sheets (pages 139–141) to students based on their readiness levels.

These activities use the Three-Story Intellect Model to differentiate types of questions. The below-grade-level students will answer Level I and II questions. On-grade-level students will answer Level I, II, and III questions. Above-grade-level students will answer Level II and III questions.

Activity Levels
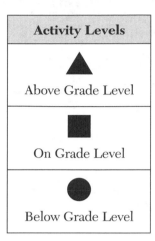
Above Grade Level
On Grade Level
Below Grade Level

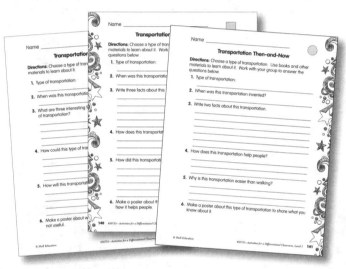

6 Students should answer questions and create their posters. The on-grade-level students should work with partners. Meet with your below-grade-level students to work with them in a small group.

7 If students finish early, they may complete the Anchor Activity.

Assessment

To assess students' understanding, ask each student if he or she can explain orally or in writing why or how one type of transportation is useful. Note whether the student completed all of the requirements for this assignment.

Anchor Activity

Have students use craft materials to create a new form of transportation or to make a current type of transportation better. They should be prepared to explain why this change or invention is needed for the future, and how it will make life easier in the future.

Name _____

Transportation Then-and-Now Pictures

Directions: Cut out these pictures. Sort them into "Then" and "Now" piles.

Name _____

Transportation Then-and-Now

Directions: Choose a type of transportation. Use books and other materials to learn about it.

1. Type of transportation:

   _____

2. When was this transportation invented?

   _____

3. What are three interesting facts that you learned about this type of transportation?

   _____

   _____

   _____

   _____

4. How could this type of transportation *not* be helpful?

   _____

   _____

   _____

   _____

5. How will this transportation change in the future?

   _____

   _____

   _____

   _____

6. Make a poster about why this transportation is useful or not useful.

Name _____

Transportation Then-and-Now

Directions: Choose a type of transportation. Use books and other materials to learn about it. Work with your partner to answer the questions below.

1. Type of transportation:

_____

2. When was this transportation invented?

_____

3. Write three facts about this transportation.

_____

_____

_____

_____

_____

4. How does this transportation help people?

_____

_____

_____

5. How did this transportation change people's lives?

_____

_____

_____

_____

_____

6. Make a poster about this type of transportation. Be sure to say how it helps people.

Name _____

Transportation Then-and-Now

Directions: Choose a type of transportation. Use books and other materials to learn about it. Work with your group to answer the questions below.

1. Type of transportation:

_____

2. When was this transportation invented?

_____

3. Write two facts about this transportation.

_____

_____

_____

_____

_____

4. How does this transportation help people?

_____

_____

_____

5. Why is this transportation easier than walking?

_____

_____

_____

6. Make a poster about this type of transportation to share what you know about it.

On the Trail

Differentiation Strategy

  Multiple Intelligences

Standards

- Students will understand what life was like for children and families "on the trail" when they moved from one part of the U.S. to another.

- TESOL: Students will use English to obtain, process, construct, and provide subject matter information in spoken and written form.

Materials

- lesson resources (pages 144–147)

- pictures of covered wagons (wagon.jpg)

- books and websites about pioneer life *(See page 167.)*

- chart paper or construction paper

- markers

- art supplies

- audio recorder

1 Ask students: How many of you have ever moved before? What was that like? What did you take with you? Tell students that they are going to study what it was like to travel a long time ago in a wagon on a trail.

2 Point out to students that when people traveled by covered wagon on the trail, they were moving to a new home. They had to take with them everything they would want in their new home and anything they would need on the trip. It was difficult for people to get supplies once they left. Display a picture of a covered wagon. Tell students that one covered wagon would hold an entire family and all of their belongings.

3 Ask students: What might need to be fixed or worked on with this covered wagon on a month-long trip? Have small groups discuss jobs on the trail. Have students think-pair-share about necessary jobs and then share out to make a class list. Brainstorm with students, thinking through the possibilities. Use any resources (textbooks, picture books, and the Internet) to help support students' understanding of life on the trail. Ask the following questions:

- What would happen if a wagon wheel cracked?

- Who would fix it?

- What would happen if the group had to cross a creek?

4 Divide the class into heterogeneous groups of three. Distribute a picture of a covered wagon, a sheet of chart paper, and markers to each group. Pose the following scenario to students:

> *Pretend your group is going on a long trip across the country to move to a new home. Think about what things you need for this trip. You will have limited space, so only choose what you really need to get to your new home safely.*

5 Have students brainstorm a list of items on their posters. Questions to ask students while they are working can include:

- What will you use to fix things when they break?

- How will you cook your food?

- What will you do if your clothes tear or get dirty?

On the Trail

6. Give groups a chance to share their thinking with the whole class. Review what life "on the trail" might have been like with students and talk about challenges that settlers might have faced while traveling.

7. Distribute copies of the *Life on the Trail* activity sheets (pages 144–146) to students. These activities focus on verbal/linguistic, visual/spatial, and bodily/kinesthetic intelligences. You can allow students to choose one activity, assign an activity to each student, or have students complete all three activities, if time permits.

   ★ **English Language Support**—For English language learners, provide the opportunity to make an audio recording of their journal activity or puppet show notes.

8. If students finish early, they may complete the Anchor Activity.

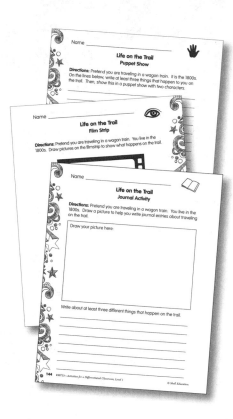

Assessment

To assess students' understanding, use the *Life on the Trail Rubric* (page 147) for each student.

Anchor Activity

Have students choose a job from the class list of possible jobs on the trail. Then, have them become an expert at that job so that they can share their learning with their classmates. Have students read about this (from resources provided) and complete a *KWL* chart.

Name _____

Life on the Trail
Journal Activity

Directions: Pretend you are traveling in a wagon train. You live in the 1800s. Draw a picture to help you write journal entries about traveling on the trail.

Draw your picture here:

Write about at least three different things that happen on the trail.

_____

_____

_____

_____

_____

_____

Name _____

Life on the Trail
Film Strip

Directions: Pretend you are traveling in a wagon train. You live in the 1800s. Draw pictures on the filmstrip to show what happens on the trail.

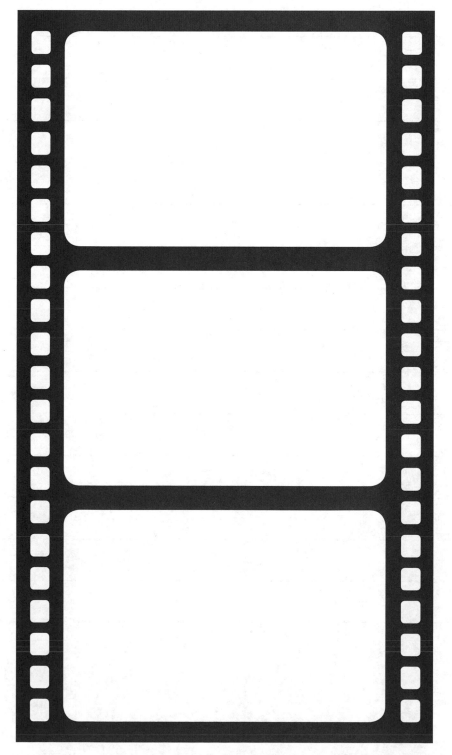

Name _____

Life on the Trail
Puppet Show

Directions: Pretend you are traveling in a wagon train. It is the 1800s. On the lines below, write at least three things that happen to you on the trail. Then, show this in a puppet show with two characters.

_____

_____

_____

_____

_____

_____

_____

_____

_____

_____

_____

_____

_____

© *Shell Education*

Student: _____

Life on the Trail Rubric

Teacher Directions: Use the rubric below to assess students' work.

Criteria	1	2	3
Participation and Discussion Earned points: _____	Student did not participate in class discussions or with his or her small group about life on the trail.	Student participated to some extent during class discussions and/or group discussions about life on the trail.	Student participated during class discussions and group discussions about life on the trail.
Content Earned points: _____	Student included only one event that might have happened on the trail in his or her final product.	Student included 2–3 events that might have happened on the trail in his or her final product.	Student included 4 or more events that might have happened on the trail in his or her final product.
Following Directions Earned points: _____	Student did not follow directions during this project.	Student followed directions only part of the time during this project.	Student followed directions all of the time during this project.
Total Points: _____ / 9	**Teacher Comments:**		

Chinese New Year

Differentiation Strategy

Tiered Assignments

Standards

- Students will know the holidays and ceremonies of different cultures.

- TESOL: Students will use English to obtain, process, construct, and provide subject matter information in spoken and written form.

Materials

- lesson resources (pages 150–153)

- world map

- pictures, videos, books, or websites about Chinese New Year (*See page 167.*)

- chart paper and markers

- sticky notes

- art supplies

❶ Ask students: What do you think about when you hear the word *holiday*? How do you celebrate the New Year? Allow students to share responses with the class. Tell students that they are going to study China and how people in China celebrate the New Year holiday. Explain that other cultures celebrate the New Year, but they do things a little differently. Display a world map and indicate where China is on the map in comparison to your country. Ask students: What do you think people in China do to celebrate New Year's Eve? Create a chart that has a column for predictions, a column for questions, and a column for facts learned.

❷ Divide the class into small heterogeneous groups. Distribute paper for each group and have them generate predictions about Chinese New Year traditions. Have groups share their ideas. Use the class chart to list the different groups' predictions. Tell each student to think of at least one question he or she has about Chinese New Year and have each student write this question on a sticky note. Add these to the class chart.

❸ Share information about Chinese New Year by using the key points below. Explain that Chinese New Year is also called Lunar New Year and that the exact date of Lunar New Year varies each year. You may wish to find out the date of the upcoming Chinese New Year to demonstrate to students that it is not celebrated on January 1, like the western New Year.

- Chinese New Year is the most important holiday in the Chinese culture.

- The celebration begins on the first day of the first month in the Chinese (lunar) calendar, and continues until the fifteenth of that month, which is the Lantern Festival.

- There are many traditions surrounding Chinese New Year. Every family cleans their house to sweep away any bad luck and make room for good luck during the New Year.

- Doors and windows are decorated with red paper cutouts with words such as *wealth* and *happiness*.

- On the eve of Chinese New Year, families have large feasts and end the night with fireworks.

Chinese New Year

4 Share any pictures and videos that you locate about Chinese New Year. Ask students to record at least one fact about Chinese New Year on a sticky note. Add these sticky notes to the third column of your class chart. Read these aloud to the class.

★ **English Language Support**—Allow English language learners to share a fact orally and record it for them, as needed. Pictures and videos will be especially beneficial to these students.

5 Distribute copies of the *Celebrating Chinese New Year* activity sheets (pages 150–152) to students based on their readiness levels. Explain the directions and explain to students that their final product will be a brochure or a poster. Tell students that pictures will help others to better understand the information.

Activity Levels
▲
Above Grade Level
■
On Grade Level
●
Below Grade Level

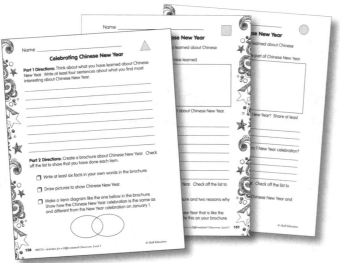

6 If students finish early, they may complete the Anchor Activity.

Assessment

To assess students' understanding, fill out the *Chinese New Year Assessment* (page 153), at the appropriate readiness level for each student.

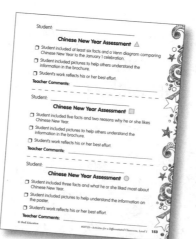

⚓ Anchor Activity

Have students choose another holiday that China celebrates (such as the Dragon Boat Festival, the Pure Brightness Festival, or the Mid-Autumn Festival). They should find out more about this holiday, draw a picture that explains it, and present it to the class.

Name _____

Celebrating Chinese New Year

Part 1 Directions: Think about what you have learned about Chinese New Year. Write at least four sentences about what you find most interesting about Chinese New Year.

_____

_____

_____

_____

_____

_____

_____

Part 2 Directions: Create a brochure about Chinese New Year. Check off the list to show that you have done each item.

☐ Write at least six facts in your own words in the brochure.

☐ Draw pictures to show Chinese New Year.

☐ Make a Venn diagram like the one below in the brochure. Show how the Chinese New Year celebration is the same as and different from the New Year celebration on January 1.

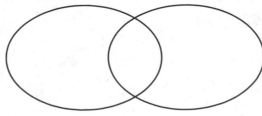

© *Shell Education*

Name _____

Celebrating Chinese New Year

Directions: Think about what you have learned about Chinese New Year.

1. Draw a picture to show what you have learned.

[ ]

2. Write five facts that you have learned about Chinese New Year. Use your own words.

_____

_____

_____

_____

_____

_____

3. Create a brochure about Chinese New Year. Check off the list to show that you have done each item.

☐ Write at least five facts in your brochure and two reasons why you like Chinese New Year.

☐ What is something about Chinese New Year that is like the New Year holiday on January 1? Write this on your brochure.

Name _____

Celebrating Chinese New Year

Directions: Think about what you have learned about Chinese New Year.

1. Draw a picture to show your favorite part of Chinese New Year.

2. What do you like most about Chinese New Year? Share at least two things.

   _____

   _____

   _____

3. What do you like most about the January 1 New Year celebration?

   _____

   _____

   _____

4. Create a poster about Chinese New Year. Check off the list to show that you have done each item.

   ☐ Write at least three sentences about Chinese New Year and what you like most about it.

   ☐ Draw pictures of Chinese New Year.

© *Shell Education*

Student: _____

Chinese New Year Assessment △

- ☐ Student included at least six facts and a Venn diagram comparing Chinese New Year to the January 1 celebration.

- ☐ Student included pictures to help others understand the information in the brochure.

- ☐ Student's work reflects his or her best effort.

Teacher Comments: _____

— —

Student: _____

Chinese New Year Assessment ▢

- ☐ Student included five facts and two reasons why he or she likes Chinese New Year.

- ☐ Student included pictures to help others understand the information in the brochure.

- ☐ Student's work reflects his or her best effort.

Teacher Comments: _____

— —

Student: _____

Chinese New Year Assessment ⬤

- ☐ Student included three facts and what he or she liked most about Chinese New Year.

- ☐ Student included pictures to help others understand the information on the poster.

- ☐ Student's work reflects his or her best effort.

Teacher Comments: _____

Alexander Graham Bell

Differentiation Strategy

 Menu of Options

Standards

• Students will know the accomplishments of major scientists and inventors.

• TESOL: Students will use English to obtain, process, construct, and provide subject matter information in spoken and written form.

Materials

• lesson resources (pages 156–159)

• books and resources about Alexander Graham Bell *(See page 167.)*

• photograph of Alexander Graham Bell (agbell.jpg)

❶ Display or distribute copies of the *Alexander Graham Bell's Sketch* activity sheet (page 156). Ask students what they think this drawing is about. List their ideas on the board. Tell students that this is a sketch of an early telephone. It was drawn by the person who invented the telephone.

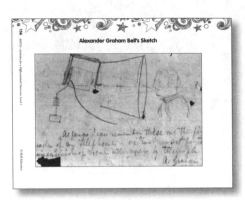

❷ Ask students to predict how long the phone has been around. Tell students that the telephone was first used on August 3, 1876, which is more than 100 years ago. Display the photograph of Alexander Graham Bell for the class and tell students that this is the man who invented the telephone.

❸ Distribute copies of the *Introducing Alexander Graham Bell* activity sheet (page 157) to students and read the text aloud.

❹ Have students work with partners to answer the following questions: What questions do you have about Alexander Graham Bell? What have you learned so far? Walk around while students are working and ask questions about their thinking. Use this information and additional resources to guide a class discussion about Alexander Graham Bell that will clarify learning and answer students' questions.

Alexander Graham Bell

5 Distribute copies of the *Alexander Graham Bell Menu of Options* activity sheet (page 158) to students. Explain the directions to students. Allow students to work with partners if they wish. Answer any questions students may have.

★ **English Language Support**—Conference individually with English language learners, asking them to restate the directions to you. Give them time to ask you questions. Assign English language learners to language-proficient partners. Encourage students to ask questions if they are unsure about something while they are working.

6 If students finish early, they may complete the Anchor Activity.

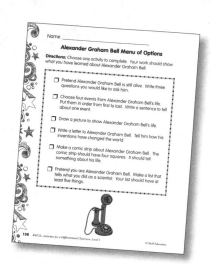

Assessment

Have students complete the *Alexander Graham Bell Self-Assessment* (page 159) to evaluate their understanding.

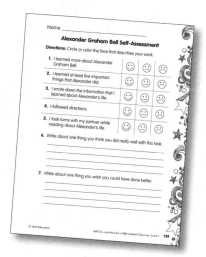

Anchor Activity

Have students brainstorm and list ideas that illustrate how Bell's telephone invention changed the world. They may include any relevant ideas, large or small, such as *the phone brought people closer together*, or *the phone made "911" possible*. If time allows, have students share their information with the class.

Alexander Graham Bell's Sketch

Name _____

Introducing Alexander Graham Bell

Alexander Graham Bell was a very curious child. Alexander began learning about new things. His mother began to go deaf. So, Alexander learned about sound. He learned how to send a sound message through a **telegraph**. A telegraph is a machine that taps out a code. Then, someone turns the code into words that make a message. At first, Alexander did not know how to do this. But a famous scientist helped him find out. Alexander kept trying. He finally invented the first telephone. He made the first telephone call on August 3, 1876. The telephone that he invented changed the world!

Name _____

Alexander Graham Bell Menu of Options

Directions: Choose one activity to complete. Your work should show what you have learned about Alexander Graham Bell.

☐ Pretend Alexander Graham Bell is still alive. Write three questions you would like to ask him.

☐ Choose four events from Alexander Graham Bell's life. Put them in order from first to last. Write a sentence to tell about one event.

☐ Draw a picture to show Alexander Graham Bell's life.

☐ Write a letter to Alexander Graham Bell. Tell him how his inventions have changed the world.

☐ Make a comic strip about Alexander Graham Bell. The comic strip should have four squares. It should tell something about his life.

☐ Pretend you are Alexander Graham Bell. Make a list that tells what you did as a scientist. Your list should have at least five things.

Name _____

Alexander Graham Bell Self-Assessment

Directions: Circle or color the face that describes your work.

1. I learned more about Alexander Graham Bell.	☺	😐	☹
2. I learned at least five important things that Alexander did.	☺	😐	☹
3. I wrote down the information that I learned about Alexander's life.	☺	😐	☹
4. I followed directions.	☺	😐	☹
5. I took turns with my partner while reading about Alexander's life.	☺	😐	☹

6. Write about one thing you think you did really well with this task.

_____

_____

_____

_____

7. Write about one thing you wish you could have done better.

_____

_____

_____

_____

American Symbols

Differentiation Strategy

Leveled Learning Centers

Standards

- Students will know the history of American symbols such as the national flag.

- TESOL: Students will use English to obtain, process, construct, and provide subject matter information in spoken and written form.

Materials

- lesson resources (pages 162–165)

- children's books about the American flag *(See page 167.)*

- art supplies

- audio recorder and listening center materials *(optional)*

Preparation Note: Prepare three centers with the following materials. It is recommended that you record the text on *The Pledge of Allegiance* (page 164) activity sheet for students to listen to at Center 3. These centers can be completed over several days.

Center 1—Copies of *The United States Flag Today* activity sheet (page 162); crayons; writing paper

Center 2—Copies of *The Betsy Ross Flag* activity sheet (page 163); writing paper

Center 3—Copies of *The Pledge of Allegiance* activity sheet (page 164); crayons; drawing paper; recording of *The Pledge of Allegiance (optional)*; listening center materials *(optional)*

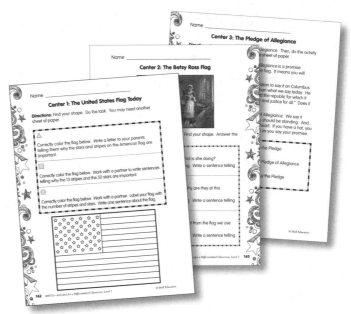

1 Begin by showing students *The United States Flags* activity sheet (page 165). Talk about how the flag has changed over time. Have students compare these flags with the flag we use today that has 50 stars.

American Symbols

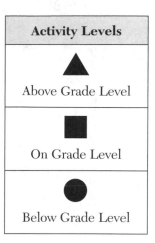

2 Read a children's book about the history of the United States flag. Talk about key points, including that Betsy Ross sewed the first American flag in May of 1776. Today the flag has 13 stripes to represent the original 13 colonies that became the first states to join the United States. The United States flag also has 50 stars that represent the 50 states that now make up the United States of America. The flag has some nicknames that include Old Glory, Stars and Stripes, and Star-Spangled Banner. June 14th is Flag Day, which is a day to honor the flag and what it means to Americans.

3 Have students write or draw two interesting things that they learned and then share these with a partner.

4 Assign students a shape that corresponds to their readiness levels. Explain that as they rotate through the three different centers, they need to complete the activity that matches that shape.

5 Divide the class into three groups and have each of the groups begin at a different center. You may allow students to rotate as they finish their work or ring a bell to signal the next rotation.

6 Walk around the room to observe and assist students with their center activities.

★ **English Language Support**—Have a recording of the reading portion on the *Pledge of Allegiance* activity sheet (page 164) at the corresponding center so that these learners can listen to the text as they follow along.

7 If students finish early, they may complete the Anchor Activity.

Assessment

Ask students questions as they work in the centers in order to determine whether the lesson objective was met.

Activity Levels

▲
Above Grade Level

■
On Grade Level

●
Below Grade Level

Anchor Activity

Have students write about the American flag. Have them locate interesting facts about it in picture books or on the Internet. Staple together five sheets of paper to create mini-booklets for students to publish a book about the flag. Have students share these books when they are done.

Name _____

Center 1: The United States Flag Today

Directions: Find your shape. Do the task. You may need another sheet of paper.

▲

Correctly color the flag below. Write a letter to your parents telling them why the stars and stripes on the American flag are important.

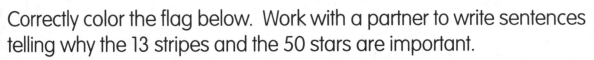

◼

Correctly color the flag below. Work with a partner to write sentences telling why the 13 stripes and the 50 stars are important.

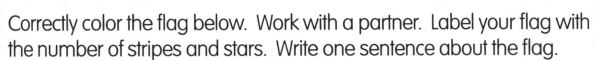

●

Correctly color the flag below. Work with a partner. Label your flag with the number of stripes and stars. Write one sentence about the flag.

Name _____

Center 2: The Betsy Ross Flag

Directions: Look at the painting above. Find your shape. Answer the questions on another sheet of paper.

1. Look at the woman on the right. What is she doing?
2. Choose one person from the painting. Write a sentence telling what he or she might be saying.

1. Who do you think these men are? Why are they at this woman's house?
2. Choose two people from the painting. Write a sentence telling what they might be saying.

1. How is the flag in the painting different from the flag we use today?
2. Choose two people from the painting. Write a sentence telling what they are saying.

Name _____

Center 3: The Pledge of Allegiance

Directions: Read about the Pledge of Allegiance. Then, do the activity that matches your shape on a separate sheet of paper.

A pledge is a promise. *The Pledge of Allegiance* is a promise to America. It means you will respect the flag. It means you will honor America.

Francis Bellamy wrote it. He wanted children to say it on Columbus Day. The pledge he wrote was shorter than what we say today. He wrote, "I pledge allegiance to my flag and the republic for which it stands, one nation indivisible, with liberty and justice for all." Does it sound different?

Both children and adults say the Pledge of Allegiance. We say it when we raise the flag. As you say it, you should be standing. And, you should put your right hand over your heart. If you have a hat, you should take it off. You should face the flag as you say your promise.

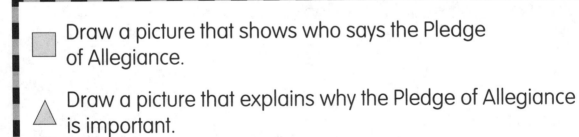

■ Draw a picture that shows who says the Pledge of Allegiance.

▲ Draw a picture that explains why the Pledge of Allegiance is important.

● Draw a picture that shows how we say the Pledge of Allegiance.

Name _____

The United States Flags

Grand Union Flag 1775

Betsy Ross Flag 1777

13-Star Flag 1777

Star-Spangled Banner Flag 1795

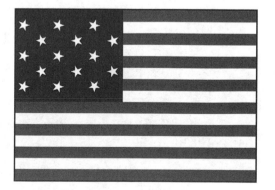

Bess, J. 1997. *Teaching well and liking it: Motivating faculty to teach effectively.* Baltimore, MD: Johns Hopkins University Press.

Brandt, R. 1998. *Powerful learning.* Alexandria, VA: Association for Supervision and Curriculum Development.

Bruner, J. 2004. *Toward a theory of instruction.* Cambridge, MA: Belnap Press of Harvard University Press.

Costa, A. L., and R. Marzano. 1987. Teaching the language of thinking. *Educational Leadership* 45: 29–33.

Gardner, H. 1983. *Frames of mind: The theory of multiple intelligences.* New York: Basic Books.

———. 1999. *Intelligence reframed: Multiple intelligences for the 21st Century.* New York: Basic Books.

Jensen, E. 1998. *Teaching with the brain in mind.* Alexandria, VA: Association for Supervision and Curriculum Development.

Kaplan, S. N. 2001. Layering differentiated curriculum for the gifted and talented. In *Methods and materials for teaching the gifted*, ed. F. Karnes and S. Bean, 133–158. Waco, TX: Prufrock Press.

Olsen, K. D. 1995. *Science continuum of concepts: For grades K–6.* Black Diamond, WA: Books for Educators.

Sprenger, M. 1999. *Learning and memory: The brain in action.* Alexandria, VA: Association for Supervision and Curriculum Development.

Teele, S. 1994. Redesigning the educational system to enable all students to succeed. PhD diss., University of California, Riverside.

Winebrenner, S. 1992. *Teaching gifted kids in the regular classroom.* Minneapolis, MN: Free Spirit Publishing.

Additional Resources

Where books and websites are referenced in lesson materials lists, some suggestions for these resources are provided below. Shell Education does not control the content of these websites, or guarantee their ongoing availability, or links contained therein. We encourage teachers to preview these websites before directing students to use them.

Page 34—Retelling

Bemelmans, Ludwig. *Madeline*. New York: Penguin, 2000.

Hoban, Russell. *A Bargain for Frances*. New York: HarperCollins, 1992.

Penn, Audrey. *Chester Raccoon and the Big Bad Bully*. Terre Haute, IN: Tanglewood Press, 2009.

Page 40—Reading for Fluency

Rasinski, Timothy and Lorraine Griffith. *Texts for Fluency Practice, Level A*. Huntington Beach, CA: Shell Education, 2005.

www.freereading.net *(click decodable passages)*

Page 46—Poetry

Fujikawa, Gyo. *A Child's Book of Poems*. New York: Sterling, 2007.

Silverstein, Shel. *Where the Sidewalk Ends*. New York: HarperCollins, 2004.

Webb, Kaye. *I Like This Poem: A Collection of Best-Loved Poems Chosen by Children for Other Children*. New York: Puffin Books, 1999.

Page 94—Weather

Branley, Franklyn M. *Sunshine Makes the Seasons*. New York: Collins, 2005.

DeWitt, Lynda. *What Will the Weather Be?* New York: Collins, 1993.

Rabe, Tish. *Oh Say Can You Say What's the Weather Today? All About Weather*. New York: Random House Books for Young Readers, 2004.

Page 106—Plants

Cole, Joanna. *The Magic School Bus Plants Seeds: A Book about How Living Things Grow*. New York: Scholastic Paperbacks, 1995.

Fowler, Allan. *From Seed to Plant*. Danbury, CT: Children's Press, 2001.

Iasevoli, Brenda. *Time for Kids: Plants!* New York: HarperCollins, 2006.

Page 136—Changes in Community

Bingham, Caroline and Trevor Lord. *Big Book of Transportation*. New York: DK Publishing, 2006.

Page 142—On the Trail

Gregory, Kristiana. *Across the Wide and Lonesome Prairie: The Oregon Trail Diary of Hattie Campbell*. Pine Plains, NY: Live Oak Media, 2005.

Kudlinksi, Kathleen V. *Facing West: A Story of the Oregon Trail*. New York: Puffin, 1996.

http://oregontrail.org

www.pbs.org/weta/thewest/places/trails_ter/oregon.htm

Page 148—Chinese New Year

Marx, David F. *Chinese New Year*. Danbury, CT: Children's Press, 2002.

Zucker, Jonny. *Lanterns and Firecrackers: A Chinese New Year Story*. Hauppauge, NY: Barron's Educational Series, 2003.

www.history.com *(search Chinese New Year)*

Page 154—Alexander Graham Bell

Kulling, Monica. *Listen Up! Alexander Graham Bell's Talking Machine*. New York: Random House Books for Young Readers, 2007.

MacLeod, Elizabeth. *Alexander Graham Bell*. Kids Can Press, 2007.

Mara, Wil. *Alexander Graham Bell*. Danbury, CT: Children's Press, 2003.

Schaefer, Lola M. *Alexander Graham Bell*. Mankato, MN: Capstone Press, 2003.

http://kids.yahoo.com/reference/encyclopedia

Page 160—American Symbols

Binns, Tristan Boyer. *The American Flag*. Portsmouth, NH: Heinemann Library, 2001.

Clinton, Catherine. *Hold the Flag High*. New York: Katherine Tegen Books, 2005.

Lewison, Wendy Cheyette. *F is for Flag*. New York: Grosset and Dunlap, 2002.

Thomson, Sarah L. *Stars and Stripes: The Story of the American Flag*. New York: HarperCollins, 2003.

Contents of the Teacher Resource CD

Lesson Resources

Page	Lesson	Filename
24–27	Memories	pg024.pdf
30–33	Words Are Everywhere	pg030.pdf
36–39	Retelling	pg036.pdf
42–45	Reading for Fluency	pg042.pdf
48–51	Poetry	pg048.pdf
54–57	Descriptive Words	pg054.pdf
60–63	More-or-Less Story Problems	pg060.pdf
66–69	Fractions!	pg066.pdf
72–75	Measurement	pg072.pdf
78–81	Geometry	pg078.pdf
84–87	Extending Patterns	pg084.pdf
90–93	Time	pg090.pdf
96–99	Weather	pg096.pdf
102–105	Where Does the Moon Go?	pg102.pdf
108–111	Plants	pg108.pdf
114–117	How Do Birds Eat?	pg114.pdf
120–123	Scientists Observe and Experiment!	pg120.pdf
126–129	Water Changes	pg126.pdf
132–135	Family Life and Community	pg132.pdf
138–141	Changes in Community	pg138.pdf
144–147	On the Trail	pg144.pdf
150–153	Chinese New Year	pg150.pdf
156–159	Alexander Graham Bell	pg156.pdf
162–165	American Symbols	pg162.pdf

Image Resources

Page	Image	Filename
82	clover	clover.jpg
82	tricycle	tricycle.jpg
100	moon phases	moonphases.jpg
106	plant	plant.jpg
114	eagle	eagle.jpg
114	finch	finch.jpg
114	hummingbird	hummingbird.jpg
114	woodpecker	woodpecker.jpg
142	covered wagon	wagon.jpg
154	Alexander Graham Bell	agbell.jpg
156	Alexander Graham Bell Sketch	bellsketch.jpg
157	Bell Engraving	bellengraving.jpg
163	Betsy Ross	betsyross.jpg
165	Betsy Ross Flag	rossflag.jpg
165	Grand Union Flag	grandunion.jpg
165	Star-Spangled Banner	starspangled.jpg
165	13-Star Flag	13stars.jpg

Teacher Resources

Title	Filename
Answer Key	answers.pdf
Sight Words List	sightwords.pdf
T-chart	tchart.pdf
Three Column Chart	threecolumn.pdf
Time Line	timeline.pdf
Venn Diagram	venn.pdf